Comfort Food
for Your Soul

Dawn Hall
with Hope Lyda

HARVEST HOUSE PUBLISHERS

EUGENE, OREGON

Cover by Left Coast Design, Portland, Oregon

Cover image © Anneli Holmgren

Published in association with the literary agency of Allen O'Shea Literary Agency LLC, 615 Westover Road, Stanford, CT 06902.

COMFORT FOOD FOR YOUR SOUL
Copyright © 2004 by Dawn Hall with Hope Lyda
Published by Harvest House Publishers
Eugene, Oregon 97402
www.harvesthousepublishers.com

Library of Congress Cataloging-in-Publication Data

Hall, Dawn.
  Comfort food for your soul / Dawn Hall with Hope Lyda.
    p. cm.
  ISBN 0-7369-1334-3 (pbk.)
  1. Spiritual life—Christianity. 2. Providence and government of God. I. Lyda, Hope. II. Title.
  BV4501.3.H346 2004
  248.8'6—dc22   2004008989

Printed in the United States of America

04 05 06 07 08 09 10 11 / BP-MS / 10 9 8 7 6 5 4 3 2 1

To my two wonderful daughters, Whitney and Ashley.

Not only were life's challenges difficult for your daddy and me, but also for you. You both paid a high price. I wish it had not been so hard on you. I did the best I could every moment of every day, yet the childhood you had was not the one I fantasized I would offer my children. There were many sacrifices required to make your daddy's dream a reality. All he wanted was to live to see his little girls become young ladies. Thank the Lord his dream came true.

Please know the price you paid did not go unnoticed or unappreciated. I hope you have feelings of self-respect, admiration, and gratification in knowing that the choices your daddy and I made for all four of us were not only for his behalf, but all mankind. I pray, as your daddy did, that the healing of his brain cancer through Dr. Stanislaw Burzynski's treatments and care will provide research and knowledge to help many other people.

You daddy was a true miracle, and his committed faith shaped our story of trusting in God and receiving His comfort. You both are a part of the continuing story of God's goodness.

I love and cherish you tremendously. Thank you for your love, kindness, grace, mercy, and understanding. I hope someday you will be blessed with daughters as wonderful as you. I thank God for you daily!

Acknowledgments

Thank you to LaRae Weikert and Carolyn McCready, who did not give up on pursuing me to write this story. I've never told either of you this, but at first I didn't think you were legitimate. Me? A small-town girl being sought out to write for a national publisher a *real book?* Something that wasn't a cookbook? I'd never done that before. It sounded too good to be true. Thank you for seeing in me what I didn't see in myself. I appreciate your perseverance and your belief in my possibilities.

Special gratefulness for Hope Lyda, my editor, who made sense of my non-sense and cleaned up my ramblings. It had to be especially challenging working with a first-time writer. Thank you for your patience and for being gentle with me.

Many thanks to Coleen O'Shea, my literary agent, for taking care of my best interest. The work you do on my behalf helps me provide for my family without having to wear the many hats and put in the grueling, long hours self-publishing once demanded. I am forever grateful to you for the relief your help has been. I will also be eternally grateful to JoAnna Lund for introducing us to each other.

I have to say, I am impressed with the professionalism and quality in which Harvest House Publishers takes care of me as one of their authors. Thank you, everyone, for making me feel a welcomed part of your publishing family, and for all of the hard work, energy, and time! You each do a fantastic job in your respective areas. I appreciate you!

Contents

*Let them give thanks to the Lord for his unfailing
love and his wonderful deeds for men, for he satisfies
the thirsty and fills the hungry with good things.*

PSALM 107:8-9

God's Recipe for Beginnings

Many are the plans in a man's heart, but it is the LORD's purpose that prevails.

PROVERBS 19:21

In the beginning was the Word, and the Word was with God, and the Word was God. He was with God in the beginning. Through him all things were made; without him nothing was made that has been made. In him was life, and that life was the light of men.

JOHN 1:1-4

The fear of the LORD is the beginning of wisdom; all who follow his precepts have good understanding. To him belongs eternal praise.

PSALM 111:10

In all my prayers for all of you, I always pray with joy because of your partnership in the gospel from the first day until now, being confident of this, that he who began a good work in you will carry it on to completion until the day of Christ Jesus.

PHILIPPIANS 1:4-6

One

Starting from Scratch
Every Story Has a Beginning

Because I spend much of my time in the kitchen cooking, experimenting with ingredients, and sharing recipes, I think of God as my Master Chef. He adds many spices and seasonings into my life mixture. Some I did not want to be a part of my personal recipe, others I welcomed. But as God creates me into the person He plans for me to be, everything blends together perfectly in His hands.

I am hoping you will be able to taste the many flavors of life from the bittersweet to the startling sour to my personal favorite—the ooh-la-la, absolutely delicious. Give me a full, rich, flavorful life over a plain, tasteless, undercooked one anytime.

My story is a good example of how truth can sometimes be stranger than fiction. I have faced hardships I would never have imagined. But as a result of the tough times, I have also experienced the depths of God's love in a way I would never have imagined. God is a God of compassion, and His mercy is more fully understood when you reach places of sorrow or pain.

In 1994 the love of my life, my high school sweetheart, and my husband of ten years was diagnosed with brain cancer. Our lives were instantly turned inside out. The pursuit of alternative treatments was expensive and, of course, held no guarantees. Yet our hope resided in our Lord, and we moved ahead with the decision to do whatever we could to give Tracy the best chances for survival. After more than six years of living with this disease and trying to maintain a revised version of normal living for our young family, Tracy's cancer was gone. As we were just beginning to understand this miracle and rebuild our lives physically and emotionally, my beautiful and still-fragile husband walked over to our neighbor's for a visit, fainted, and hit his head on the cement. He would die just a while later in the hospital from hemorrhaging.

How can a miracle be followed by such sorrow? To lose Tracy in such an unexpected way after all we had done to beat the cancer was surreal. Instead of planning how our new life would be without cancer, I was planning my husband's funeral. *Not this way. Not after all of this struggle.* The loss seemed unbearable. I had imagined my girls losing their father to cancer for quite some time, but to have his life end this way, and on the cusp of hope, felt so unfair. It was difficult to grasp and consider a reality—but it was.

And praise God that the other part of my reality was a deeply rooted faith in my Provider. Tracy was buried wearing a sweatshirt that read "God's Property." Perfect. He truly was and is the property and the child of his Father. This was my comfort. I knew, without a doubt, that the Lord my husband and I both loved, served, and depended upon continued to pour out His love and mercy on all of us who faced life without Tracy.

Tracy and I experienced many beginnings together—from the day we met to our first date to our marriage and our life as parents—and we were blessed with a sense of how beginnings offer renewal and a chance to see God's hand bring us through good times and bad. Then on a day in May 2001, I had to face a beginning without Tracy but still with God. My legs were shaky and my heart was broken, but I was with the Healer and He was showing me a way through this time in my life, just as He always did. I reached for His hand and asked Him to be my strength, my comfort, and my foundation. I invited Him to lead me and my girls into the next part of our lives because I could not manage alone. For more than six years I had been giving over control of my life to God's hand. So when Tracy was gone, I understood the good that had come from something as terrible as cancer. Tracy's journey had shown us how to love the Lord in all circumstances and at all times. Tracy's journey had shown us how the Lord provides peace that passes understanding.

Life is full of challenges. Bad things happen to the good, the bad, and everyone else in between. The difference for me—compared to someone who doesn't know and love God—is that I don't have to go through life alone. God is my hope, my refuge, my everything. I would rather live through many difficulties in the comfort of His arms than live without strife and without Him.

I would never have chosen to go through all my family has been through, yet I am so thankful for all the good that has come from it.

It's a God Thing

Many times I have felt weak, flawed, and unable to move forward. Even as a child of God, I find myself asking the question, "How on earth will He make something of this fallible life I am offering Him?" But, of course, it is not "on earth" but "in heaven" that the power exists to turn weakness into strength, failure into success, and grief into joy.

When I am in the midst of trials, I turn to God's Word for sustenance and direction. Opening up my favorite Bible, the worn pages in Genesis hold words of significance and hope. God made Adam from the earth. "The LORD God formed the man from the dust of the ground and breathed into his nostrils the breath of life, and the man became a living being" (Genesis 2:7). God created a being in His image out of a pile of dirt. Can you imagine? While I know God is not a genie in a bottle, I do understand He is powerful and caring and compassionate. He didn't blink, wink, or nod and await the POOF that precedes any fantastical display of power. God chose to create, form, and shape humans by merging ingredients of earth and heaven. His Spirit entered a small pile of dust, and a soul was formed. God is so good.

It is no accident that the beginning of God's Word includes the reassuring story of man's origin. The premise is essential for our understanding of the gifts of creation and grace. God—and only God with a capital "G"—can take the ordinary and turn it into the extraordinary.

I want to share how this miracle has taken place in my life so you can carry this hope along on your own journey. Are you facing physical pain? Are you trying to wrap your understanding around a loss too big to bear? Maybe you long for comfort from your Lord to handle ordinary circumstances. For many, daily life can overwhelm them and hold their hope hostage in much the same way as a tragedy will. I believe this is true because we were made to need God and His strength for our every circumstance…big or small.

Because this book presents my story in brief glimpses, I want to provide you with a chronological order of significant events. After all, I wouldn't give you a list of ingredients without sharing the entire recipe!

1984   Tracy Wayne Hall, the sweetheart of my youth, and I get married.

1987   Our first daughter, Whitney, was born against all odds.

1988   Ashley is born.

1991   The groundbreaking takes place for our built-from-scratch home. We call it Cozy Homestead.

1994   At age 32, Tracy is diagnosed with cancer. His brain tumor is the size of a baseball. He has surgery and is paralyzed on his left side. Radiation takes its toll and causes him to be tired and sick frequently.

1995   We look into alternative treatments. The one we select costs more than $3500 a month. Taking a leap of faith, we decide this is what we need to do.

1996   We self-publish my first cookbook, *Down Home Cookin' Without the Down Home Fat*, to cover the treatments. The success of the book and the amazing support of friends, strangers, and the community is evidence of God's provision and care.

1999   Initially Tracy is doing very well and even returns to work full-time for a few months. We start attending Waterville Open Bible Community Church, a local church, to shorten our drive time and to develop a stronger outreach in our immediate community. By August Tracy takes a turn for the worse, and we initiate further changes in his medication and treatment.

2000   Cozy Homestead is engulfed in flames in February; remodeling efforts and God's goodness restore our family home later that year. In June I enter the Mrs. Ohio pageant and the next day Tracy and I celebrate our sixteenth anniversary by renewing our vows.

2001   Our miracle—Tracy is cancer free and is removed from the hospice care list. As a family we vote to return to our home church Calvary Assembly of God. Just two days after that decision to "go home," Tracy faints while standing outside and hits his head on cement. The resulting hemorrhaging is substantial, and my dear husband goes home to be with the Lord. The funeral is a celebration of Tracy's life, faith, and the God who continues to provide for those Tracy has left behind.

This timeline represents my story. And my story, just like your own, is a God thing. God created our lives from scratch, and He has given us what we need to discover the vibrant, abundant life He intended. I encourage you to use a journal to record your responses to the "What's on Your Plate?" questions throughout this book. This action will nudge you to reflect on a deeper level, and your written account of comfort and faith will be a source of encouragement along your journey.

I pray you will learn to trust the Creator as I have learned to trust Him. When your life is changing, when you face pain or heartache or uncertainty, know that God is ready to create, shape, and form the beginning of a new story in your life. And He will see it, and you, through to the end.

COMFORT FOOD FOR THOUGHT

God began a good work in you.

Chicken Vegetable Soup

14 cups water
4 chicken-flavored bouillon
    cubes
4 whole bay leaves
1 16-ounce can spinach
1 16-ounce can asparagus
1 16-ounce can sliced stewed tomatoes
1 16-ounce can creamed corn
1 16-ounce bag of frozen oriental-style mixed vegetables
1 16-ounce bag of frozen mixed vegetables
1 teaspoon sweet basil
½ teaspoon black pepper
1 tablespoon garlic powder
1 tablespoon garlic salt
2½ to 3 cups chicken breast (approximately 3 10-ounce chicken breasts)

Bring chicken to boil in water. (If not using boneless chicken, boil for about 5 minutes. Remove chicken from water and debone, if necessary.) Remove fat from chicken water by pouring chicken water through a strainer filled with ice positioned over a large pot. The ice will collect the fat from the water. If needed, this process can be repeated 2 or 3 times. Add remaining ingredients to chicken water. Once again, bring to a boil.

Very important: Remove bay leaves before eating.

Serves: 29   Fat Grams: 1.4   Calories: 89

Note: If you like brothier soup, simply add water or canned chicken broth.

This soup reheats nicely, and you will have plenty to put aside to savor when you are in the mood for a bowl of comfort. Each recipe in this book provides you with lots of servings to feed your family, friends, or to set aside for days when a ready-made treat will lift your spirits.

What's on Your Plate?

1. How is life changing for you right now? Can you view it as a beginning in any way?

2. Identify the "God things" in your current circumstances. I encourage you to write these down. They can offer you encouragement along the way.

3. What truths can you rest in? Look around you and claim the things that offer you hope, stability, strength, and nourishment.

4. An extraordinary life does not mean problem-free or sorrow-free living. It is a life that leads us closer to God's heart and is shaped by trials and victories alike. How is your life extraordinary right now?

5. Usually we don't choose our struggles, but we do have choices while in the midst of them...choices that can feed the good work God is doing in us. What are some choices you can make that support His good work?

God's Recipe for Life

Love and faithfulness meet together; righteousness and peace kiss each other.

PSALM 85:10

Know therefore that the LORD your God is God; he is the faithful God, keeping his covenant of love to a thousand generations of those who love him and keep his commands.

DEUTERONOMY 7:9

Finally, brothers, whatever is true, whatever is noble, whatever is right, whatever is pure, whatever is lovely, whatever is admirable—if anything is excellent or praiseworthy—think about such things.

PHILIPPIANS 4:8

Commit to the LORD whatever you do, and your plans will succeed.

PROVERBS 16:3

You were taught, with regard to your former way of life, to put off your old self, which is being corrupted by its deceitful desires; to be made new in the attitude of your minds; and to put on the new self, created to be like God in true righteousness and holiness.

EPHESIANS 4:22-24

Two

Gathering Ingredients
It Takes a Lot to Make a Life

God has given us all the right ingredients and directions for our lives through His Word, the Holy Spirit, and our faith experiences. Unfortunately, we sometimes find it easy to substitute these gifts with the wrong ingredients. Faithfulness is replaced by inconsistent behavior based on our whims and desires. Obedience is replaced by following our will instead of His. Trust is exchanged for doubt. Then, when we face trials too difficult to handle on our own, we wonder why we are struggling. Along the way we made so many substitutions that we completely changed the ingredients God planned for us to have in that very moment of life.

Even though I don't like to admit this, I often learn things the hard way. (I'm sure my mom is tickled pink to finally hear me admit to this.) I recall driving down our long country road delivering meals to others in need. I took a selfish moment to count up my brownie points and said to God half-jokingly, "There is no way You could ever give back to me all the meals I've made for others." What a fool I was. Even if I was somewhat kidding, I was really expressing a limited view that is easy to substitute for God's limitless grace. As I made those deliveries and many others out of a heart of compassion, I was also keeping track subconsciously. Self-righteousness took the place of godly righteousness.

So there I was, doing Christianly things and the big lesson still evaded me. I was doubting God in that moment. Such a humbling lesson...a lesson I would not fully learn until Tracy's cancer diagnosis. Before my husband's illness I loved and served the Lord, but I was confusing God's character and wisdom with my very human, wrong ingredients.

And wouldn't you know, for four months after Tracy's surgery I did not make one meal. Not one. My family was flooded with more delicious home-cooked meals, desserts, and breads than we could eat. We were so inundated with offerings prepared graciously by friends, family, and neighbors that we had to even turn down or give meals away so they wouldn't spoil in our refrigerator. Humility is one of the good ingredients God has us gather along the journey of struggle or hardship.

With each lesson we learn, we draw closer to understanding and accepting God's heart for us because we have the ingredients that true faith requires. When the next hardship comes along, we can rest in that deeper, wider, more meaningful relationship we have with the Lord. While there are many faith ingredients, the most influential in my life have been those of love and faithfulness. At times I felt these coming directly from God. In other moments I understood that I or my family was supposed to stand strong in one of them in order to wait out or wade through a circumstance. But whether I was receiving or giving, these mainstays fed our spirits when nothing else could.

The Ingredient of Love

Tracy and I had a fairy-tale love. We met in the seventh grade in the Springfield school system of Holland, Ohio. Years later my loving husband, Tracy Wayne Hall, confessed, "I knew when I first met you in Mrs. Phlagar's seventh grade math class that I wanted to marry you someday." I too had a crush on him from the moment I saw him. He had beautiful coloring, with rosy lips that always looked as if he'd just moistened them. His cheeks were sun-kissed with hues of pink that made his blue eyes sparkle even bluer. Tall, handsome, and always in denim jeans, Tracy's body was strong from years of cycling. His large, beautiful hands were just like my Grandpa Schaefer's, and I always remembered Grandpa saying he needed big hands so he could take good care of Grandma. I liked that idea.

It took many years for very shy Tracy to muster the courage to talk with me and ask me out, but by our junior year we were going steady. I was the homecoming queen and he was my escort. I was a cheerleader and he was the captain of our varsity basketball team. It felt like a match made in heaven.

Even with such strong feelings for Tracy, I was concerned that he had never really dated anyone else. My birth father never dated anyone except my mother, and that relationship ended in divorce. I wanted to learn from what I thought were my father's mistakes. So after graduation we decided to spend some time apart, in God's Word and willing to date other people. Tracy promised that he would, so I decided to move to Kentucky in order to give us some geographic distance for a while. With more than a few tears, I loaded my orange Ford Pinto with all my earthly belongings and headed to Lexington, where I worked as a waitress. My love for Tracy remained strong, but I knew this time was important for us both. After only three months of separation, Tracy asked me to marry him. When I asked if he had been dating other people as he had agreed to do, he replied, "Don't worry. It's all been taken care of." Years later I discovered this response was a no disguised as a vague yes. He said he didn't need to date anyone else to know I was the one he wanted to marry.

We married on June 29, 1984. God blessed us with a deep, caring love for one another—a love that would serve us well as we built a life together and as we faced trials while gathering more of God's ingredients.

The Ingredient of Faithfulness

The words of a song we sang in church left an impression on me as a young girl: "God is faithful, so faithful to me." I understood that *we* are called to be faithful, but I did not grasp how God could be faithful to me. Maybe as immature Christians we are so caught up in the do's and don'ts of our faith that we miss the bigger picture...that we are engaged in a relationship with the living God. This relationship isn't one-sided. It isn't just about us and our behavior; it is about recognizing and accepting those ingredients God gives us along the way. Sometimes He extends the ingredient directly, and other times He acts in our circumstances.

As a woman who had always desired to have children, news that my endometriosis might prevent me from becoming pregnant was heartbreaking. But Tracy and I were hopeful and prayerful, and God blessed us with a pregnancy. Then, just three months after we celebrated the news of a baby, I was in a car accident. To this day I thank God that the new seatbelt law had just come out or I wouldn't have been wearing mine—but I was, and it saved me and the baby.

The sounds and emotions of the accident are as vivid as the day I was rear-ended by a teenage driver—the terrible sound of screeching tires followed by a sickening crash. Everything in my car went flying forward. My vehicle was hit so hard that the back-seats were dislodged and fell onto the floor.

I was so worried about the baby that I didn't immediately realize how much pain I was in. My unborn child was okay, but I had severe whiplash that would create intense pain throughout my pregnancy and for many years after that. Tracy, my mom, and my sister Kellie took shifts taking care of me once I was home. Even though I knew in my mind I could walk, my legs would give out under me and I would fall. It was very scary. There were times I would cry out to God and beg Him to take the pain or take me. Of course, God wanted me to get back to the life He had planned for me.

In April 1987, I went into labor with Whitney. For more than 20 hours Tracy was a terrific labor coach to a wife stuck in a neck brace. It was all worth it. As soon as I saw Tracy hold his precious child I understood he was meant to be a father. I remember telling people, "Isn't it wonderful when your husband, your lover, your best friend, and the father to your children are all the same man?"

I wanted to be the best mom I could be. Knowing that I might not be able to ever have another child, I did all I could to endure my pain so I could care for my daughter. But my body was still struggling to heal from the accident and finally rebelled with severe migraines. One episode was so bad that our neighbor two doors down could hear me screaming. Tracy called for an ambulance, and as the EMT lifted my sweat-drenched body, the look in my husband's eyes revealed how much he suffered at the sight of my pain.

"I'm sorry, Tracy. I'm so sorry," I cried. We both knew it wasn't my fault, yet I felt so bad for all he was being put through. He never once complained.

"Someday you'll be taking care of me," he said.

"Don't say that, honey," I said.

"It's true, Dawn. Someday I really do think you will be taking care of me. I just have this gut feeling." He had said this several times before, and every time the words left his mouth I cringed with the thought of him ever experiencing pain. My desire from that day on was to get healthy and keep my family safe.

I kept Tracy's sense of the future at bay while we focused on being good parents and the joy of parenting. A year and a half later our second miracle girl, Ashley, was born on Veterans Day. We were so blessed to beat the odds by having these two babies. And while we knew God had shown us His love and faithfulness in bringing about our little family, we did not know how important those ingredients would be as we faced bigger trials.

We are so blessed to love a God who knows what we will need and when we will need it. I look back to this time in our lives with such gratitude. As you walk through a time of uncertainty, may you look back and claim those ingredients God has blessed you with along your own journey. Discover how God has sprinkled your life with the essential gifts of love and faithfulness.

COMFORT FOOD FOR THOUGHT

God gives us faith ingredients along the way.

Harvest Pudding

16 egg whites
2 ⅓ cups skim milk
⅓ cup NutraSweet Spoonful
    (or ⅓ cup sugar)
1 12-ounce can of evaporated skim milk
½ cup brown sugar, packed
1 teaspoon vanilla
½ teaspoon lite salt
½ teaspoon cinnamon
½ teaspoon ground cloves
8 slices lite (40 calorie) fat-free wheat bread, dried
    (best if laid out the night before to dry)
½ cup raisins
1 medium apple, chopped thinly, with skin on (approximately ¾ cup)

Preheat oven to 350°. Spray a 9 x 13-inch pan with nonfat cooking spray. Beat together egg whites, milk, NutraSweet, evaporated milk, brown sugar, vanilla, salt, cinnamon, and ground cloves. Mix bread, raisins, and apples into the egg mixture. Pour into prepared pan. Bake for 40 to 45 minutes or until a knife inserted near the center comes out clean. Serve warm with spicy cream topping.

Spicy Cream Topping:
1 package Dream Whip
½ cup cold milk
½ teaspoon cinnamon
½ teaspoon ground cloves

Prepare according to package directions and refrigerate unused portions.

Serves: 12   Fat Grams: .2   Calories: (with sugar and no calorie
                                sweetener) 129 (with sugar
                                only) 150

What's on Your Plate?

1. Think through a few ingredients you know God has given you during your lifetime. How do they bring you comfort in this moment?

2. If your heart is heavy and you do not have the strength to find the ingredient of hope in your current circumstance, allow yourself to just rest in God. Know that His care is sufficient for your needs right now.

3. Today, give to God a burden that is weighing you down. Ask Him to turn it into a life-giving ingredient as you release your worry to His care.

4. How do you see God caring for you? Find something in the days ahead that gives you a glimpse of Him watching over you: a kind word from someone, a surprise offer of help, a special moment of prayer, a good night's sleep. Look for His hand on your life.

God's Recipe for Trust

Yet you brought me out of the womb; you made me trust in you even at my mother's breast. From birth I was cast upon you; from my mother's womb you have been my God.

PSALM 22:9-10

In him our hearts rejoice, for we trust in his holy name. May your unfailing love rest upon us, O LORD, even as we put our hope in you.

PSALM 33:21-22

Commit your way to the LORD; trust in him and he will do this: He will make your righteousness shine like the dawn, the justice of your cause like the noonday sun.

PSALM 37:5-6

Three

Stirring It Up
When God Moves in Your Life

When the family doctor calls after office hours, from his cell phone, on a holiday weekend, it is a pretty good indication that something is not right. In our case, something was seriously wrong.

I trusted our doctor completely and took comfort in his voice and in knowing that he truly cared for our family, not only as patients of his, but as people. Still, I knew that even the nicest doctors do not make casual calls, and my entire body froze. I asked the question I did not want to ask. "Is everything okay?"

"Dawn, you'd better sit down," he said gently. I sat on the edge of our bed and listened as he calmly delivered the most difficult news. "Tracy's MRI came back. He has a spot on his brain. He needs to be admitted to the hospital first thing in the morning so we can run more tests."

"What do you mean? What kind of spot? How big of a spot?"

He tried to answer my questions as honestly as he could in a reassuring tone that made me feel he was avoiding dropping all the bad news on me at one time. "You could come into the hospital tonight, but it's late and I need to make some contacts with doctors who have expertise in this area. Come in first thing tomorrow morning."

"Okay," I said maintaining my composure as much as possible. "Thanks for calling." As soon as I heard him hang up I began crying. For nearly a month I had been certain something was wrong and had begged, pleaded, and even nagged Tracy to get checked. But Tracy was beyond a reluctant patient. He was as mule-headed as they come, and, like most men, took pride in the fact that he rarely went to the doctor's office. But this time, even he knew something was wrong. He described the pain as "getting struck by lightning," and when it hit, he'd reach for something to regain his balance. He was scared of the unknown and had hoped it would disappear. But soon a numbness on his left side was too hard to ignore. And when he started taking naps after work, we all knew something was up.

I'm the kind of person who wants to immediately fix anything that goes wrong. I want to get the bad part over with so I can move on. And one day I erupted. We were shopping with the girls when I realized my husband was holding on to the grocery cart for dear life with his head tilted.

"It feels like I'm walking on the side of a steep hill," he said.

"That's it, Tracy. I've had enough. I don't care if you get mad at me or not. I'm getting you in to see the doctor."

I don't know if his fear of my response that day outweighed his fear of the unknown, but he agreed. A sense of relief came over me, and for the first time in weeks I felt as though I could breathe. Finally we were going to find out what was wrong.

When Life Changes

After that first call from the doctor, I had a churning in my stomach and in my spirit—a feeling I would experience often as pain and suffering stirred in our lives. I knew this was just the beginning of a difficult road, and I prayed we had the faith to keep us strong and united as we faced the unknown together.

I allowed myself to quietly cry for a few minutes, and then I headed down the hallway. When Tracy saw my face he asked what was wrong. It was all I could do to not begin bawling. I was so frustrated that he had waited to seek help, and I was so afraid of the unknown. My feelings were an inner tornado of compassion for him and fear for our family.

"I'm fine," I whispered. After all we've been through I now realize there are a million levels of fine. That day, my level of fine was at its lowest. I really meant "I am still standing but scared." I stopped midway in the hall and called out to him. "Can you come here?" I didn't want the girls to see I'd been crying. I wasn't sure how he was going to handle this information or if he even wanted the girls to know what was wrong.

I felt his right hand on my shoulder as he tried to comfort me, still not knowing at all what was upsetting me.

"That was the doctor on his car phone…"

Before I could even tell him what the doctor had said, Tracy revealed his fear. "When he ordered my CAT scan and MRI, I knew he thought something was seriously wrong with me." I reached over and held his hand and told him what I knew. He didn't say a word. We were both so numb. He was in a state of total belief and total disbelief at the same time. His worst fear had come true, yet it seemed unbelievable.

How could this be happening? He looks so healthy. You never think something like this will happen to you. In unity with anyone who has ever experienced such news in the past, or who will in the future, the truth that you never really think it will happen to you is indeed universal. There is almost a comfort that comes with understanding that others have crossed over this line to go on to face their struggles with faith and with fear. With hurt and with hope.

We agreed to talk to the girls right away because they would be concerned when we checked Tracy into the hospital. But my strong husband continued to stare at the carpet, numb and lifeless. I squeezed his hand three times, meaning "I love you." It was one of our little ways of communicating without speaking. Usually he'd squeeze my hand back four times, symbolizing "I love you too." No reply.

"Tracy, everything is going to be okay."

"Yeah, I know," he said without much feeling. It was from this moment on that I realized the word "okay" also has at least a million different levels of meaning.

Letting God Have It

Giving God a piece of your mind is probably not something you learned about in Sunday school or during a typical sermon. But during the hard times, I would bet that you have done this. If you haven't, I strongly recommend it. I believe in coming to God with reverence. I also believe that it is important to come to God when we are raw—when we discard polite salutations and break through the inclination to offer unfeeling, rote sayings. Your Creator knows your heart. When you need to shout out to God, do not hold back. It could be the start of true dialogue about your situation.

I think I have always been pretty open with God, but on the day we received the scary news I really let God have it. The fear in Tracy's eyes as he explained to the girls the uncertainty of his health was more than I could bear. My emotions welled up in me. No, they tore through me. I had to get out of the house right then.

I went out to the back of our five acres and I yelled, I screamed, and I bawled as loud as I could for as long as I could— and it was all directed at God. I really let Him have a piece of my mind. The worry that had been building since Tracy's first signs of trouble was now pouring out of me. This venting and crying was between me and God. I was so glad we lived in the middle of nowhere so I could yell and scream at the top of my lungs without neighbors filing reports of a "wild woman" in their midst. I threw sticks, kicked the ground, and hit a tree or two. I needed to rid myself of this unbearable, emotional pain. It was my way of grieving. I had to deal with my negative feelings so I could move on to what was ahead.

When you stand face-to-face with your hurt, God is stirring in your life. As I shouted out to Him in the middle of our acreage, I felt alive in my pain. And I felt a sense of intimacy with my Lord because I was being so honest. Weary from crying, I then slipped into shouters-regret mode and apologized to God. His acceptance embraced me. I knew He understood. Whenever you are sharing your difficulties with God, He knows your thoughts and feelings even before you express them to Him. But the act of revealing our feelings to Him is important because it lets us move on. Twelve-step programs have a phrase that applies to this. They call it: Let go and Let God!

After I had my fit and vented my full rage at God for allowing this to happen, I finally was quiet enough to listen to Him. Certainly He could have spoken to me first, but I was in no state to hear Him. I wanted to speak my piece first. There is no need to deny the truth of the negative feelings we experience. It is important to acknowledge them to God and to ourselves so we can move on. Otherwise, painful feelings eat away at our energy. And those feelings keep stirring up our trouble because we are unable to make room for God's peace within our hearts.

In the stillness of our woods I emptied myself and was ready to listen. God told me, "I am going to use this most challenging situation to give praise and glory to My name." Having this revealed to me gave me great peace and comfort. I went inside to share this peace with Tracy. Together we believed it was truth from God.

COMFORT FOOD FOR THOUGHT
God is in control.

Au Gratin Soup

By my mom,
Wendy Oberhouse

3 boxes au gratin potatoes
    (your favorite brand); set cheese aside
1 head fresh cauliflower
1 bunch broccoli
1 packet onion soup mix, dry
1½ quarts skim milk
1 teaspoon rubbed thyme, dried
1 teaspoon marjoram leaves, dried
2 teaspoons parsley
3 packets of cheese from the boxed potatoes
8 slices fat-free American cheese
2 teaspoons cornstarch (optional)
salt to taste
pepper to taste

Put the first four ingredients into a 6-quart Dutch oven. Cover with water (approximately 4½ quarts) until all ingredients are covered. Bring to a boil, reduce heat, and simmer until tender, about 20 to 30 minutes. Add remaining ingredients and simmer 5 minutes or until cheese is melted.

If it's not as thick as you would like it, add 2 teaspoons cornstarch mixed with ¼ cup milk.

Serves: 30   Fat Grams: .5   Calories: 94

Invite a group of loving friends or family members over to share a bowl of soothing goodness with you. They can even stir in favorite added ingredients, such as chopped turkey, ham, or chicken.

What's on Your Plate?

1. What difficult situations in your life do you believe God wants to use for His glory?

2. Have your own "wild woman" experience to express your hurts and frustrations. Choose a safe place to unload your feelings, and then listen for God to speak to your heart.

3. Do you believe God is in control of your situation? Think of Him taking control of your churning emotions. Feel Him stirring in your spirit with the power of peace.

4. How can you give God praise and glory through your challenging times?

5. If it is difficult to see through your current pain, talk to someone who has been through a struggle similar to your own. Begin to see how God is moving in your life by witnessing His faithfulness in the lives of others.

God's Recipe for Provision

If that is how God clothes the grass of the field, which is here today, and tomorrow is thrown into the fire, how much more will he clothe you, O you of little faith!

LUKE 12:28

You are my hiding place; you will protect me from trouble and surround me with songs of deliverance.

PSALM 32:7

May integrity and uprightness protect me, because my hope is in you.

PSALM 25:21

"Because he loves me," says the LORD, "I will rescue him; I will protect him, for he acknowledges my name. He will call upon me, and I will answer him; I will be with him in trouble, I will deliver him and honor him."

PSALM 91:14-15

Sustain me according to your promise, and I will live; do not let my hopes be dashed.

PSALM 119:116

LORD, you have assigned me my portion and my cup; you have made my lot secure. The boundary lines have fallen for me in pleasant places; surely I have a delightful inheritance.

PSALM 16:5-6

Until now you have not asked for anything in my name. Ask and you will receive, and your joy will be complete.

JOHN 16:24

Four

Making Bread
Watching God's Provision
Take Shape

"But how does it rise and grow like that?" When I first discovered how to make bread as a young girl, I was full of questions. I would peek under the white dish towel draped over the bowl holding two small mounds of dough—the beginnings of bread, so they said. *Not much bread*, I thought, disappointed with the outcome of the mixing and kneading efforts. Doubt always mixes a bit of pessimism into our efforts. And I had not yet seen proof of how the blending of certain ingredients would cause mere blobs to rise into spectacular loaves.

But, sure enough, with each passing minute measured by the tick of the kitchen clock and my growing anticipation, the dough was rising. And by the time I was permitted to place those loaves in the oven, pessimism had given way to optimism and a seed of belief in provision had been planted. Certainly, I did not quite learn such a mature lesson at that point. I was more focused on coating slices of thick, dense bread with jam. But now, years later and with many failures and successes in the kitchen and in life, I recall the miracle of watching bread rise and how it gave rise to spiritual truth. God's provision, like the ingredient of yeast, is not only enough...it is part of the plan.

The cost of life's trials can be emotional, physical, spiritual, and sneaky ol' financial. Sometimes our trials are brought on by money problems, but occasionally our life-and-death situations deliver us a bill that seems impossible to pay. We can wear a Christian smile and say, "God will provide," but when we go to our checkbook, we are still asking, "But how, Lord. How?" And just as I watched those insignificant bits of dough with skepticism, I have also stared at insufficient bits of money and questioned how God's special ingredient of provision would unfold.

Financial struggles often go hand in hand with situations involving health conditions, family problems, job difficulties, and so on. I will share a little about my family's financial situation, but I don't want money talk to keep you from embracing what this chapter is really about—trusting God's provision for every aspect of our lives. Whether we are screaming at God out in the woods or silently weeping on our pillow, God hears the question "How, Lord?" He will show you how. And I will give you a story of hope for you to hold.

But How, God?

As we gathered information about Tracy's type of cancer, we were directed to Dr. Burzynski and his experimental nontoxic brain cancer treatments. Though excited about the success of his work in the field, the price tag of $20,000 to get started and $3500 each month was nevertheless a little daunting. I believed in God's provision, but even with great faith ingredients in my life from past times of struggle and victory, I had times of doubt. I asked God "how" more than a few times. Prior to this adventure, those figures would have seemed impossible. In fact, if they had been attached to anything else we would have laughed and said, "So much for that idea." But there was no laughter, only a spark of hope. And that was worth becoming a believer in miracles.

I spent many restless days and nights standing on my foundation of worry. I prayed. I talked to Tracy. I prayed some more. I cried. I doubted. I ranted. I shouted. And then, just like that day in the woods, I finally listened. God was trying to give me answers.

"Use the book," I heard Him say as clear as day.

"What book?" I asked, knowing full well what He meant. For years I had been creating recipes. And each time I wrote one out, I tossed it on top of the refrigerator and referred to it as the cookbook I was writing. But I was never serious about it.

"God, I just *told* people I was writing a cookbook. It is more of a pipe dream; I never really intended to pursue it."

"Use the cookbook."

I started listing all my best excuses. You know, the ones that keep you from doing what you dream of doing. *But God, I don't know how to type or use a computer. I don't know a thing about publishing. And who else other than friends and family would ever buy something I created?* I was an aerobics teacher and facilitator for WOW (Watching Our Weight groups), and my students had encouraged me to do a cookbook as a way to share my meal ideas. It's funny how ridiculous our dreams seem or easy it is to push them aside during "normal" times. It often takes extraordinary experiences to shake us up or wake us up.

And then God assured me that if churches could use cookbooks as fundraisers, I could too. If you wonder what God's voice sounds like, it sounds like your own voice. How did I know it was God and not my own thoughts? Because there is no way I would have ever attempted to do such a thing.

We had $3000 remaining in our savings, and I was only making $6.25 an hour as an assistant activities director. My thought was we can either spend it all on one treatment and then be left with nothing, or I can try to invest that amount in cookbooks and keep reinvesting until I raised enough money to pay for multiple treatments. I knew it was a long shot, but I felt it was what God wanted me to do. I was simply following His leading.

One of the students in my W.O.W. class, Diane (who was also a cousin of Tracy's), offered to type all the recipes. I went to an art store, bought clip art of different foods, and glued it onto the typed recipe pages. A local printer printed 1000 paperback cookbooks.

God's Provision Is His Plan

I'll never forget how afraid I felt driving home with our minivan filled with a thousand cookbooks. "You're nuts!" I told myself. "How are you ever going to sell a thousand cookbooks?" I gave a box of books to every friend and family member who was willing to help me sell them for five dollars each. To my surprise, we sold 1000 cookbooks in five days, and 18,000 cookbooks in ten weeks. It was a God thing. My goal was to raise $100,000 for Tracy's treatments.

When the fundraiser was over, I started looking in the paper for a new job. I figured people were just buying my recipes out of respect for someone trying to earn their own way for cancer treatments as opposed to asking for a handout. In my limited view of God's provision, each buyer gave us a donation and I gave them a cookbook as a thank-you gift. I was not seeing the bigger picture.

Two weeks after the fundraiser was over, we kept receiving phone calls asking for those fast-and-easy low-fat recipes. Most people couldn't remember the title of the book: *Down Home Cookin' Without the Down Home Fat*. They simply wanted the "fast-and-easy recipes."

To meet the demand for my product, Tracy and I borrowed every single penny of equity we could against the small ranch home we had built ourselves only three years earlier. We doubled the size of our house payment, Tracy was unable to work, and I was responsible for this debt. Talk about pressure. Doubt and faith were at play in my heart, and I was once again a young girl peeking at bits of dough with concern.

After suffering a setback by going to a printer that was not up to the task, I hired a professional printer and we were finally in business. I entered that book into a contest, and it was selected as one of Ohio's Best of the Best Cookbooks by Quail Ridge Press and the 1996 Best Cookbook of the Year by North American Book Dealers Exchange.

After a considerable amount of time, hard work, and lots of prayer, I paid off the loan, got caught up with medical bills, and could finally breathe again.

I look back on the beginning of this journey with a sense of blessing and humility. God asked me to bring to His table an offering of myself. I handed over scraps of paper with recipe ideas that represented years of creativity, energy, experimentation, and silly fun. I really did not have a plan for any of those random ideas. But God did. He included this part of my life in a way I could never have imagined. And just like dough with a touch of yeast, His provision continues to grow and rise. God calls me to use the rewards of those "silly" scraps of paper to share about my life, my faith, and His provision through speaking engagements, books, talk shows, and my own cooking show.

I am in awe that He continues to give to me and use my offering to serve Him in wonderful ways. Living each day in and under God's hand becomes an ongoing, ever-changing experience of grace and humility. I was looking for financial stability, and He was trying to shape something much bigger.

I do not know where you are along your own journey, but I pray you are finding your way to faith in God's provision. I do not know your specific situation, but I do know the Lord and His care for His children. There has been proof, somewhere and sometime in your life, of His ability to care for you. Today might be one of those days you are peeking beneath the white cloth and shaking your head...waiting and waiting for something to come of your efforts.

I offer you encouragement and empathy right now. I will watch the clock with you, but I will not be counting the minutes because I have doubt; I will be waiting to witness what God is planning to do with those efforts you have made. I am excited for you to see how His provision will turn your offerings into a spectacular life.

COMFORT FOOD FOR THOUGHT

God's provision is enough,
and it is part of a bigger plan.

Mmm! Mama Mia! Bread

1 package yeast
1½ cups warm water
1 teaspoon salt
1 tablespoon sugar
2 cups whole wheat flour
2 cups self-rising flour
½ cup liquid Butter Buds
2 teaspoons garlic salt
2 teaspoons basil
2 teaspoons oregano
½ cup grated Parmesan cheese

Preheat oven to 425°. Dissolve yeast in warm water. Add salt and sugar, and stir until dissolved in the water. Add both kinds of flour to water mixture. Turn the dough onto a lightly floured surface and knead it for about five to ten minutes or until dough is smooth and elastic. Spray two jelly roll pans with nonfat spray. Divide the dough in half and place in pans. Roll out dough to the edges of each pan with rolling pin. Spread ¼ cup of liquid Butter Buds onto each pan of dough, and then sprinkle with 1 teaspoon garlic salt, basil, oregano, and ¼ cup Parmesan cheese. Bake for 15 to 20 minutes or until crust is nice and brown. Serve warm.

Serves: 24   Fat Grams: .8   Calories: 81

What's on Your Plate?

1. How has God shown evidence of His provision in your life? Let these glimpses of His care give you comfort in times of need.

2. When have you felt led by God to follow through with something you thought was silly? Did you do it, or did you let doubt get in the way?

3. In what ways do you feel God is using your offerings?

4. If financial worries are a part of your struggle, and "making bread" has caused you to doubt what God can do, spend time each day giving Him thanks for what He will do in your life and circumstances. Pray for His provision to take shape and for the ability to see that provision when it rises up in your life.

5. This might feel like a time when dreams are being put off...but maybe God is giving you new dreams or new opportunities to pursue other than those you have carried with you over the years.

God's Recipe for Wholeness

Now choose life, so that you and your children may live and that you may love the LORD your God, listen to his voice, and hold fast to him.

DEUTERONOMY 30:19-20

For physical training is of some value, but godliness has value for all things, holding promise for both the present life and the life to come.

1 TIMOTHY 4:8

Dear children, let us not love with words or tongue but with actions and in truth. This then is how we know that we belong to the truth, and how we set our hearts at rest in his presence whenever our hearts condemn us. For God is greater than our hearts, and he knows everything.

1 JOHN 3:18-20

The brother in humble circumstances ought to take pride in his high position. But the one who is rich should take pride in his low position, because he will pass away like a wild flower. For the sun rises with scorching heat and withers the plant; its blossom falls and its beauty is destroyed. In the same way, the rich man will fade away even while he goes about his business.

JAMES 1:9-11

Five

Burning the Biscuits
When You Are Distracted from God

As a cook who loves to experiment in the kitchen—and as a cook who has Adult Attention Deficit Disorder—it is easy for me to become so caught up chopping, stirring, and blending over here that I completely forget about what's in the oven over there. Oh my. Disaster.

During my most intense "workaholic" days, I was too busy to enjoy what I was doing at any given moment...even if it was a hobby or special activity. I helped people. I served my family and my church. I was active in the community. But I was operating out of two dangerous philosophies: "Treat others better than yourself" (my distorted version of the Golden Rule) and "Get the job done and look ahead to what you have to do next."

Are you juggling a few things right now? I understand how hard it is to stop focusing on the many needs that surround you. "Let us fix our eyes on Jesus, the author and perfecter of our faith" (Hebrews 12:2). Keep your focus on Him. When you do, you will see the depths of compassion in His eyes. You will see your situation through the love of God. And those millions of things to do will suddenly emerge from the shadows and you will see them for what they are…distractions. Yes, we are meant to love others and to serve the body of Christ, but God also wants to provide for you and your needs. Once you are centered in Him, you are better able to serve others and your family, and tend to your heart and spirit.

I can hear the voice of rebellion now. It used to speak to me all the time when I first started to feel God's care for me as His child. So many of us believe, as Christians, that self-care undermines our role of servant. I think about growing up and watching my mother in action. In deeds of kindness to others she was probably only outdone by Mother Teresa. My mom was the epitome of unselfishness. But her greatest attributes can also be her greatest faults, because she gives at the expense of her own health. I am definitely my mother's child, and I followed in her footsteps up until a couple of years ago when, in the kitchen of life, I was burning too many biscuits. Caught up in other needs around me, I left my needs unattended.

I was a people pleaser to the point that I also did things at the expense of my family. I cannot tell you how many times I would be grouchy, impatient with my children, or irritable with Tracy because my do-it-all efforts made no room for my daily requirements of rest and nurturing. Tracy and I had what I refer to as Superman and Superwoman Syndrome. We were foolish that way.

Lessons often arise in our trials. Some are meant to be discovered later, during the time of restoration and healing. But some make themselves known quite clearly in the moment. The one that stood out for Tracy and me is how easily we can be distracted by our own pursuits and good intentions. And as we grow more scattered, more divided, and more exhausted, we lose sight of God's plan.

Tracy and I lived a very active life together. We were both geared toward doing more. And while we were building a simple life on some levels, we were also following tangents in order to earn and save money, create a special home and future for our family, and keep up with the demands of life. I would ask him, "Honey, please don't work this extra side job." And his reply was usually, "Dawn, as soon as I get this job done I can rest." Yeah, right. We both knew another job would replace the current one. Tracy wasn't fooling anyone but himself. It was only during his illness that he acknowledged and regretted how driven he was to succeed and achieve.

This kind of thinking starts innocently enough. When we were first married, we thought we had to work all the time to get ahead. After our home was built, I realized we were caught in the madness of workaholism.

Paying Attention

My turning point was during Tracy's illness. I was so scattered. I could barely breathe. I could be standing in front of a talking person but would not hear anything they were saying. Nothing registered in my brain. I watched their lips but my mind surfed a million things to do, thought about what-ifs, and tucked away cries for help.

I was running my small business, managing the family situation, and caring for Tracy; the pressure was building. My going-through-the-motions charade was not fooling anybody. One day my assistant, Momma Liz, insisted I take the rest of the afternoon off. After much protesting, I drove to the river, parked the van, and crawled in the back to take a nap. The tremendous guilt I felt for taking that bit of time for myself reflected my state of mind...rather unhealthy. I was so weary from trying to tend to so many different areas of life that I had forgotten my needs even existed.

Before sleep could overcome me I assured myself with a dose of rational thought. *Dawn, this is ridiculous! Jesus went away for 40 days and 40 nights...you're just taking the rest of the day off.*

Now that I have some distance from that day, I realize how useless my guilt was. I have spoken to many women who are struggling in the same way. They have forgotten how to be still enough to listen to their own hearts. They hold on to the lie that they are responsible for how everything turns out. Guilt, as with all distractions, must be given over to God or it will get in the way of what He is doing in your life. Now, He can work through any obstacle—even a woman's guilt—but we miss out on the blessing, wisdom, and life He has for us if we give our offering of time and energy to guilt rather than to God.

One evening Tracy and I attended a social gathering. As we sat around with some other couples the conversation almost always turned toward the material aspects of life. People discussed jewelry, salaries, trips, and houses, and they related their goals in terms of wealth and acquisition. I don't know if we had previously ignored these kinds of conversations or if we had participated in them without realizing it, but our ease with such topics turned to unease.

We left that gathering a bit disappointed. Tracy brought it up first, and we laughed over our feelings of being fuddy-duddies so early in life. We really weren't stick-in-the-mud folks; we were simply people who had aged in our faith. We were wiser in our sense of what was most important. We didn't blame the others for joining in the talk of trivial things…after all, not long ago our turmoil and toil were geared toward material growth. But through the experience of the cancer journey, we had taken on a new perspective about life and purpose.

That day almost felt like a graduation. Tracy and I were sharing a life that had more meaning than ever before. This trial was shaping us to be better people. We weren't better than the other people at that event; we were just further along our journey. I liked that we realized this together. We praised God that Tracy's illness helped us see beyond material things. We now could pay attention to what really mattered. That day helped us understand we were partners in discovering and focusing on a deeper faith and a richer life…even if we were a couple of fuddy-duddies.

COMFORT FOOD FOR THOUGHT
When God is your focus,
your journey leads to wholeness.

Soothing Comfort Tea

1 mug water
1 tea bag of your favorite
    flavor tea
2 tablespoons fat-free half-and-half

1 to 2 envelopes noncaloric sweetener
    (I use Splenda)
1 teaspoon noncaloric flavoring
    (hazelnut, vanilla, peach, raspberry)

Put the mug of water in the microwave and cook on high for 90 seconds or until boiling hot. Remove and put the tea bag in the mug of hot water for two minutes. Remove tea bag.

Stir in half-and-half, sweetener, and flavoring, if desired. Relax and enjoy!

Serving: 1   Fat Grams: 0   Calories: 26

Sipping a delicious cup of tea is one of the best ways to become centered and focused. Tea time can be a great prelude to prayer or a time to think through the day's priorities while also resting. Begin or end your day with the comfort of tea.

What's on Your Plate?

1. What keeps your eyes off God? Take time today to look at Him. See how your Lord cares for you and your needs.

2. Spend some time gathering those scattered thoughts and emotions. Pray. Rest. Go for a walk. Listen to music. Write down those thoughts and release them from inside yourself.

3. Who supports you during difficult times? Call on those people as you need help. God has placed them in your life to help care for you.

4. What gives you comfort? Think on this and then give yourself permission to experience one of those things.

5. Evaluate guilt, material pursuits, or patterns of people pleasing, and make changes where necessary.

6. Reconnect with God during this time. Don't become distracted by fear, the drive to work more, or denial. Open up to the One who truly wants what is best for you.

God's Recipe for Community

A new command I give you: Love one another. As I have loved you, so you must love one another. By this all men will know that you are my disciples, if you love one another.

Your words have supported those who stumbled; you have strengthened faltering knees. But now trouble comes to you, and you are discouraged; it strikes you, and you are dismayed. Should not your piety be your confidence and your blameless ways your hope?

JOB 4:4-6

He died for us so that, whether we are awake or asleep, we may live together with him. Therefore encourage one another and build each other up, just as in fact you are doing.

1 THESSALONIANS 5:10-11

But encourage one another daily, as long as it is called Today, so that none of you may be hardened by sin's deceitfulness.

HEBREWS 3:13

Six

Too Many Cooks in the Kitchen
The Mess and Ministry of Others

"Nobody's perfect—that's why we have Christ." If my experiences have taught me an absolute truth, this little gem of wisdom is it. You will face plenty of moments when repeating this to yourself will serve you and your sanity well. I also find this truth to be of great comfort. It reminds me that the people I am angry with or frustrated by are doing their best. Their best might baffle or disappoint me, but when I envision that person wrapped in God's grace and trying to do what they think is right, my heart softens. Whatever I am hoping that person or group of people will fulfill in my life is a misdirected expectation. My hope is in God. And when I rightly place it in Him, the tensions I have with others seem irrelevant to my journey's purpose or needs.

Nobody's perfect. Remember that in relation to yourself as well. This truth serves as a reminder of our own fallibility and inability to handle life alone. A dominant coping mechanism in either slight or severe times of hardship is to withdraw inside oneself. Maybe others have disappointed us so much that we have trained ourselves not to ask for help or seek community. But even if there are no past bad experiences dictating our actions, withdrawing from others is an act of self-preservation. It could be our way of making our world smaller...small enough to manage. I know so many times I wanted to define my world as just Tracy's cancer or my family's emotional and financial struggle. I was determined not to have too many cooks in the kitchen who could distract me, take away more of my valuable and dwindling energy, or disappoint me. Without realizing it, I was building up walls that would later be torn down by God through other people.

Self-protection is tricky because the more you distance yourself from the love and care of others, the more likely that chasm between you and community will start to bother you. Suddenly you think of lists of people who should be stopping by or calling to see if they can help. But it is you who has chosen to remove yourself from the possibility of community and fellowship. Relying on God is our comfort. Yet when we isolate ourselves so we can mull over our difficulties and examine them with focused attention, we are not allowing others to be an extension of God's comfort. And we know God works this way. He gives us so much of what we need through the love and service of others. That is the body of Christ in action.

As you open up to experiencing God's care through others, you will also face times when people are not helpful. It never ceases to amaze me how people with good intentions can say the most hurtful things. I too have done this when trying to encourage, comfort, or console someone. My first words might be of use, but then I turn the conversation to reckless observations or become self-focused and ramble on about my own problems. Thank the good Lord for forgiveness!

When People Say the Wrong Things

Tracy and I were with some high school friends we hadn't seen in a long time. We had only been in the same room for a matter of minutes when one of these precious friends said, "You know Dawn, I think God allowed Tracy to have this cancer because He knows Tracy and you are such good Christians that you two could handle it."

I stood there dumbfounded. *Could I believe my ears? She is far too intelligent to say such a thing. Is this supposed to be her idea of a compliment?*

"I don't think so," I said nonchalantly. "What about our situation would ever inspire others to want to have a personal relationship with God?" I questioned her logic while imagining what nonbelievers could covet about our lives right now: "Oh boy, I can't wait till I am a Christian so I can go through living hell right here on earth like Tracy and Dawn!" I was thankful when the subject was changed.

If I thought that sort of comment from fellow Christians was going to be a rarity, I was dreaming. The very next morning during a lesson on faith and healing in Sunday school, a professional woman spoke in the most gentle voice words that shocked both Tracy and me. "I love Tracy and Dawn," she said facing our Sunday school teacher without addressing us directly. "And I am just being honest, so please don't take this wrong, but I really do believe there must be some sin in their life for God to have given Tracy this cancer." As if her brutal words weren't painful enough, she added verbal salt to our already burning, emotional wounds. "And I think the reason why Tracy is not healed is because he does not have enough faith."

The entire class just sat there, stunned that anybody in the name of God's love could be so heartless. This person was definitely what I would consider to be a woman of God, but I had to wonder what version of God's love she had grown up with. In my head I recited the Scripture I imagined she was basing her case on: "I tell you the truth, if you have faith as small as a mustard seed, you can say to this mountain, 'Move from here to there' and it will move. Nothing will be impossible for you" (Matthew 17:20). I was flustered and unsure how to counter her in that moment. Too many thoughts were going through my head.

Thank goodness our teacher was a wise, godly man. He replied with an answer I believe Jesus Himself would have given. "God is not a yes-man. His ways are not always our ways. There is a time and season for everything under the sun. I do not know God's plans for Tracy and Dawn, but I do know that God will be with them all the way, and He will never leave them nor forsake them. He will be their strength and refuge." The words of God spoken through our teacher eased the tension of our souls and warmed the icy barrier formed by the previously spoken words.

Tracy squeezed my hand tight as he bit his lower lip. I could feel the ache of his unspoken words penetrate. Cancer had stolen too many things from this precious man. It was not fair that his integrity should have to be compromised for a disease he did not cause, could not control, and could not cure. Up until this bout with cancer, I had seen Tracy cry only once in 15 years together. If he would have tried to defend himself, I believe he would have started to cry out of sheer frustration.

For a brief moment I imagined how Jesus must have felt up on the cross when He said, "Father, forgive them, for they do not know what they are doing" (Luke 23:34). I felt that Tracy wanted to defend his credibility as a Christian who loved and served God with all his heart, but he was unable. I gave him ample opportunity and waited patiently. I didn't want to do for my husband something he wanted to do on his own. He squeezed my hand again, this time a little firmer, and with a nod of his head I knew it was permission from him to say what we both knew had to be said; not only in our defense, but in defense of every person who has ever had a life-threatening illness or debilitating disease that is not completely healed, even though they have faith far greater than a mustard seed and prayed with all of their heart.

I spoke from my chair. "I know what verse she is talking about in the Bible. However, I have given what she has said a lot of thought. Cancer happens to the good, the bad, and everyone in between. What happened to Tracy is called life. He did not cause his illness, he can't help it, and he can't cure it. Only God can. The difference between Christians with cancer and a nonbeliever with disease is we don't have to go through this alone. Psalm forty-six tells us that 'God is our refuge and strength, an ever-present help in trouble.' He can give us the peace that passes all understanding during our times of need."

I was glad it was time for our class to be over. Tracy put his arm around my shoulders and gave me a side hug. The lady who made the comment bent over the table between her chair and ours. "I am sorry," she said. "I really didn't intend anything mean by what I said."

We shook her hand. "Don't worry about it. It's okay," Tracy said in his usual kind manner. He exhibited the same gentle strength I had admired when I first saw him in seventh grade.

When People's Words Heal

Chicken, carrots, bread... As I wandered the grocery store aisles, a warm voice interrupted my mental shopping list.

"Hi, Dawn. How are you?" a woman asked as she stepped toward me.

"What?" Her question threw me for a loop. I was used to the greeting "Hi Dawn. How is Tracy?" If anyone asked about me and the kids, it was usually after a conversation about Tracy's condition. I had never even thought twice about it until now. I explained to her why I looked so shocked, and I will never forget what she asked next.

"You see what the disease is doing to him, but do you see what it is doing to you?"

Oh my gosh! I thought to myself. S*he's right. Look at me, I'm a mess.* I ate, thought, and breathed Tracy's illness and the devastating effects of what it was doing to him, our love life, our happy family life, and our finances. I tried to maintain a sense of normalcy for our daughters, even though I knew our family situation was anything but normal. I kept the pace of a mad woman and forgot about myself along the way.

"I'm sorry, what did you say?" My thoughts had once again wandered off (as per usual at this stage of my life). It was difficult to think, let alone carry on a conversation.

She repeated herself in a kind manner.

Just a few weeks prior I had left a cart full of groceries in the middle of the supermarket because I couldn't face going through the checkout, seeing more people, and answering more questions about Tracy. And how long ago was it that I bawled on the phone to Kim, one of my best friends, that I didn't feel I could take it anymore? The only time I spent energy on makeup was Sundays for church. I was always tired and constantly felt as though I was on the verge of tears.

"I'm okay," I said in an unconvincing half whisper.

She smiled as if she knew I really wasn't. It was one of those woman-to-woman moments. Even though we didn't know each other on a personal level, she had a special gift of intuition that read me like a book.

"It's so nice of you to ask," I said. I barely knew her. I recognized her face, but to this day I cannot tell you her name.

She leaned over from her grocery cart and gave me the kind of hug a mother gives to console and comfort her child. Her hug felt good, and I wanted to stay in this person's arms forever and never be let go. I call people like her "earth angels." They appear out of nowhere, at just the right time and with just the right words, and give you just what you need just when you need it. Surely, they are heaven-sent.

"Thanks," I said, holding back sudden tears. I had been trying to keep it all together on my own. Her hug let me know that God was in total control and that no matter what everything was going to be okay.

We said goodbye, and even though our encounter was brief, that woman's kindness, insight, and comforting hug were like a soothing bowl of hot chicken noodle soup to my aching body and soul.

Misplaced Expectations

In my tired mind, I kept thinking about how much lighter our burden would be if we had some consistent family help with our monthly obligations. I could clearly see the many other things they were doing to help us, and I deeply appreciated those kindnesses, but the area of money started to take over my thoughts. There I was, foolishly thinking I knew better than God what we needed at the time.

If only I would have totally given this situation over to God, I could have saved myself so much time and energy. But I didn't...and one day the financial bondage was too much to bear and I blew up big time. I had recently asked Tracy once again to seek help from his family, but he refused. I do not fully understand why, at least I did not then. Now I understand that God had a different plan for how His provision would unfold for us. But Tracy's refusal broke my heart. So those hurt feelings were very much on the surface one day when we were visiting Tracy's family.

We sat at their big country table as Tracy shared about his recent treatments and our amount of debt. But he was just stating the facts. He wasn't at all requesting financial assistance. I just sat there...frustration building. Then Tracy's mother offered some advice, and I don't even recall what it was. It was probably perfectly good advice, but I didn't want advice. I wanted help.

"This is not a Dawn Hall issue!" I screamed, staring right at Tracy's family members. If you cringed reading this, just imagine how everyone in the room felt. But I just kept on spewing. "Everyone wants him to do the experimental treatment yet I feel the financial responsibility rest solely on my shoulders." Before I knew it, I was off on a rampage and cut loose on everything I'd suppressed for some years. Total and complete exhaustion, frustration, and rage filled my every word as I purged all of my suppressed anger.

The wrath of Dawn subsided and my pain was replaced with conviction. God is an understanding, loving parent who guides us to correct our wrongdoings so healing can take place. I immediately felt how unjust I had been. In my brokenness, I apologized. By God's grace, we worked through all of this, but not until Tracy sternly declared that such an outburst would never happen again. His folks explained that Tracy had not asked them for help. They would gladly assist us if Tracy wanted that. Meanwhile, they helped in other ways. This was not anything I did not already know. And honestly, my frustration was, at the time, about my husband not asking. I knew the situation, and I had placed unrealistic expectations on everyone involved. And I count myself as one of those victims of my expectations. I was still depending only on myself and not on God for our needs.

This was the start of my letting go and giving it all to God. This was an ongoing lesson, but something had shifted in my heart. Maybe a nervous breakdown is required sometimes before we can see clearly. I know I came close that day. The rage and deep sorrow I had held in throughout Tracy's illness came pouring out. My pain took the shape of accusation and anger. I was grieving the loss of our once-normal life, and I wanted people to blame for my indescribable sadness.

God knew I was hurting, and He was there to pick up and put together the pieces of relationship and faith. It was time for me to fully believe in what He had planned. Because I am sharing this with you in hindsight, I have the blessed opportunity to place the story of my outburst and unfair expectations alongside stories of God's faithfulness. I give Him all the glory.

Unexpected Blessings

God's care and comfort are often found in the way people make room for another person's struggle. I continue to be blown away by God's faithfulness as expressed by the actions, words, and creative ideas of others.

My folks went out on a limb and borrowed money on our behalf so Tracy could start the treatment right away. They had faith that we would be able to pay them back. At first I worried about it, but they gave with an open heart and trust in the Lord. It was my turn to believe with that same faith.

While it was sometimes painful for us to learn how to trust God for every simple detail of our life, I am thankful we had Him to trust. And trusting Him taught us to also trust others. Our eyes were opened to the amazing ways people could reach out. Time after time we witnessed God's heart through the actions and kindnesses of friends and strangers. The following are just a few examples.

Two of our best friends Kim, and Andy, organized our first fundraiser. It was a combination dance, Mexican dinner, silent auction, bake sale, and raffle. Kim has incredible organizational skills, and she put them into full throttle by pulling off this very successful event. Countless people—friends and strangers—pitched in to make it a success. Over 500 people attended and $10,000 was raised. To top it all off, my parents won the raffle and graciously donated the entire $2000 they won. It was the boost of moral support and team effort we needed to get us off on the right start.

A precious little four-year-old girl, with big hazel eyes and soft brown hair, came to us with her mother, Lynn, by her side. "I have this for you," little Ellen said, reaching out a small white cardboard jewelry box to me.

"What's this, sweetheart?"

"It's all the money I've been saving," she said. "I want you to have it."

I just stood there, speechless, with tears running down my cheeks. It was one of the most beautiful acts of loving-kindness I could imagine. "Oh, honey, thank you so much. That is so kind of you. God has given you a very special heart. Thank you." I gave her a big hug. "I promise you we will never forget this gift!" I opened the lid and saw a bunch of pennies. I smiled as I looked over at her mother. She could not have looked more proud. "You have done a wonderful job, Lynn!" I said as I gave her a hug. "I can only hope my daughters will have as loving and caring hearts as Ellen has. You are truly blessed."

Ellen's generosity reminded me of the story in the Bible in which a poor lady gives her last pennies into the offering, an act that Jesus noted. "'I tell you the truth,'" he said, "'this poor widow has put in more than all the others. All these people gave their gifts out of their wealth; but she out of her poverty put in all she had to live on'" (Luke 21:3-4).

The very first thing I did once I got home that evening was to set Ellen's little box of pennies on our dresser as a constant reminder of unselfish love. She gave every penny she had with the hope of helping Tracy live. I can't tell you how many times when I was sad or wondering how we could go on, I'd look over at Ellen's pennies and be inspired by them. It was the most generous gift of all.

The surprises and blessings just kept coming. A friend and coworker at Container Graphics organized a bike-a-thon. A person we never met who worked at the White Bear Lake Container Graphics plant in Minnesota heard of our story and organized a volleyball tournament in honor of Tracy. Women at that same plant gathered during their lunch hours and created a beautiful navy blue quilt with white bears on it. The color matched our living room perfectly, and Tracy used it all the time to help him keep warm.

Another coworker and friend organized a golf tournament, and the Container Graphics Corporation offered to match up to $15,000. And sure enough, the tournament raised that much money. We were in awe. And the blessings just kept coming.

My Aunt Brenda Delong from Florida came up with the clever idea of donating an entire ten-piece miniature Beanie Baby set still in their McDonald's packaging to our family to raffle off with the proceeds going to Tracy's medical fund. People truly were shining with inspiration and God's goodness. Everywhere we turned, His love was showered on us in the most creative and passionate ways.

While there are times when facing others is difficult, God calls us to give people a chance. They might overwhelm you. They might say the wrong things. But there are some people whom God is calling to be strong and obedient in ways that serve His plan of provision for you. And you never know what God is trying to do in that person's heart as they offer help or comfort. This is how our Creator connects us to one another and to Himself.

COMFORT FOOD FOR THOUGHT

God teaches and reaches us through others.

Taco Salad

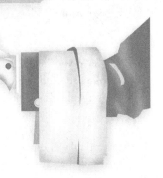

1 pound hamburger
1 envelope taco seasoning mix
¾ cup water
2 large heads of iceberg lettuce,
    torn into bite-sized pieces
8 ounces fat-free shredded cheddar cheese
4 fresh tomatoes, diced
1 medium onion, chopped
8 ounces fat-free French salad dressing
    (use more if desired)
48 low-fat tortilla chips, crushed

Brown hamburger and drain any juices. Add taco seasoning and water. Bring to a boil. Reduce heat. Simmer for 15 minutes. Remove from heat and set aside to cool.

In a very large bowl toss lettuce with cheese, tomatoes, and onion. Toss the seasoned taco meat, tortilla chips, and salad dressing in salad right before serving. You don't want to put the last four ingredients in the salad too soon before eating or the lettuce will become wilted and the tortilla chips will become soggy.

If desired, you can use the seasoned taco meat warm or cool. I would encourage you NOT to put the meat in warm unless you are going to eat the salad immediately.

Serves: 6   Fat Grams: 3.16   Calories: 243

What's on Your Plate?

1. Have you experienced a time in your life when God did for you (through others) what you were unable to do for yourself?

2. How have you helped someone? Think about how you felt when you followed God's gentle prodding to reach out to another person. God is also leading someone in your direction.

3. Are you able to replace your unreal expectations with God's good plan?

4. Are you letting Jesus carry you during this time? Give yourself completely to Him and let Him lift you up and carry you forward when you need it most.

5. If someone has harmed you with reckless words, give the person and the words over to God. Replace them in your mind with God's Word: "For he has not despised or disdained the suffering of the afflicted one; he has not hidden his face from him but has listened to his cry for help" (Psalm 22:24).

God's Recipe for Help

Help me, O LORD my God; save me in accordance with your love.

PSALM 109:26

May your hand be ready to help me, for I have chosen your precepts. I long for your salvation, O LORD, and your law is my delight.

PSALM 119:173-174

But you, O Sovereign LORD, deal well with me for your name's sake; out of the goodness of your love, deliver me. For I am poor and needy, and my heart is wounded within me.

PSALM 109:21-22

But the Lord stood at my side and gave me strength, so that through me the message might be fully proclaimed and all the Gentiles might hear it. And I was delivered from the lion's mouth.

2 TIMOTHY 4:17-18

Seven

Life as a *Sous*-Chef
Working Beside the Master

Sunday was our favorite day of the week because it was our family day. We were committed to preserving this day even when life became hectic or when the girls complained about missing an activity with friends. Our busy weeks caused us to hold more strongly to this time of unity and togetherness. Looking back, I am thankful we stuck to this because the girls now have many memories of their dad and of our family sharing time together. They will know family is the most important priority.

Our Sunday routine did not vary much. We attended church together and then usually headed home, where a lunch I had placed in the slow cooker that morning was ready to serve. The girls would help set the table as I popped savory biscuits into the oven to round off our meal. Usually we were all tired from the week's hustle and bustle, and a delicious Sunday nap would be a part of the leisurely day.

One cold February Sunday the ground was covered with inches of hard icy snow. The sky was glorious, filled with thick puffy clouds floating ever so lightly in the bright blue heavens. As

I turned down our long curvy driveway after the tranquil drive home from church, the image of smoke billowing from our chimney was a comforting scene. Our cozy little homestead welcomed us from its nesting place among nature's splendor.

After a satisfying dinner, Tracy and the girls decided to retire to their beds, but I wanted to relax and enjoy some quiet time to myself with a book. "Honey," Tracy said before he went to lie down, "make sure you open some windows a little bit in this living room. It's eighty degrees in here, but only about sixty-five degrees in the bedrooms. Make sure you tell the girls to keep their doors open so their rooms will warm up."

Soon the house was enshrouded in peace and quiet. A beautiful roaring fire in the fireplace beckoned me to the living room, where I snuggled into the couch cushions and the warmth of a quilt. Instead of reading the book in my hands, my thoughts drifted. I found myself reflecting on the blessed life we had in spite of all our hardships.

Yes, our life was hard, but God was good. I was so thankful that I did not view this as an either/or statement. I know many people who say that life is hard; therefore, God is not good. Or life is easy; therefore, God is good. Our trust in God's care protected us from such conditional faith. Even in the midst of adversity and signs of Tracy's declining health, we were still able to have the peace that passes all understanding. Such genuine peace surely was a God thing.

We had to keep on doing what we had been doing the last five years...ever since disease had become a part of our lives. We had to keep our eyes totally focused on God, and believe without a shadow of a doubt that He was going to use our situation to give Himself praise and glory, and that good was going to come from our challenges. We had no room to be anything but optimistic and hopeful because God was by our side.

Hours passed by. I'd fallen asleep on the couch. Tracy walked into the great room holding onto the hallway to help support his uneven balance. "Honey, that fire smells awfully hot." It did smell hot, but that was typical. "Better turn the blowers to the fireplace on," he suggested as he carefully sat himself down on the couch.

"It is time for our show," I said. "I'll make some popcorn." Every Sunday evening all four of us enjoyed watching our favorite program as a family. We'd turn off all the lights and savor the taste of popcorn in the room that was usually off-limits to food. Both girls were still sleeping as I set a bowl of fresh, hot popcorn on the end table next to Tracy.

Wanting to make the room as cozy as possible, I leaned over to turn on the fireplace blower then headed into the kitchen to get drinks for everyone. Within seconds, a huge flood of flames jumped out of the blowers and onto the walls with a great force. The flames let out a scream. The fire was as loud and vicious as it was hot and scary. Tracy tried to stand up to fight for the home he'd built with his very own hands and immediately fell to his knees.

"Call 911 right now!" I called out to Whitney, who was just entering the living room. At this point I was throwing tall glasses of water onto the fireplace blowers and thinking I pretty much have the fire under control, but I wanted to call 911 just in case. I had no clue what I was dealing with behind those burning walls.

Ashley was trying desperately to help her father stand, but she was too small. "Whitney, I need help!" Ashley cried. "I can't get Dad up." As fast as lightning Whitney was by her daddy's side. The three of them rallied together with all their might and were able to get Tracy back up to the chair and then in standing position.

I made the call for help. My heart was racing. I was in a panic but trying to stay as calm and collected as I possibly could. The emergency operator had a lot of specific questions that I tried to answer, but when your house is on fire the last thing you want to do is stand with a stationary phone in your hand and give out information. I told Whitney to get the cordless phone and answer the operator's questions. Tracy yelled for me to get the fire extinguisher, so I ran to the pantry where we kept it. I couldn't focus on anything. I heard Tracy's voice shout "It's down on the floor on the left side!"

I was frozen. It was the oddest thing. Then all of a sudden I felt this presence behind me, guiding, and directing me. I thought it was Tracy. I could feel the presence directing me to the fire extinguisher under a pile of stuff. I was in such a mad rush that my brain was unable to make heads or tails of the extinguisher. The presence showed me how to use it.

My heart sank as I tried to put out the flames and realized what I was witnessing: the loss of our home. Ever since Tracy's diagnosis I had done my absolute best to not lose our home to financial troubles. My every effort was spent to protect us from this one thing. And here I was now physically fighting a battle for our house.

I fought that fire with everything I had in me to the very last breath. I could not have fought it any harder or any longer. I'll never forget hearing the girls begging for me to get out. "Mom, it's just a house!" I remember Whitney screaming. But it wasn't just any house to me. It was the house their daddy had built for them. And in the face of Tracy's severe illness, I could not bear the thought of losing this part of him. To this day I am beyond grateful that the entire structure did not go up in flames.

I did not realize that Tracy was not beside me until a couple of days afterward when we were sharing with friends the story of the fire. Once I had settled from the shock of it all, I was able to sit down and rationally think through the frightening event. I realized what I thought was the presence of Tracy by my side in the pantry was not Tracy at all. It couldn't have been. He was standing outside with the assistance of our daughters. But I can vividly recall the comfort and reassurance I felt in those moments. God was beside me.

The Lord is beside us when our life is figuratively or literally aflame. By studying His Word and His ways, we are a *sous*-chef to the Creator. We study His recipe for life and faith and blend that with our daily living. We seek His approval and are quick to give Him praise for our accomplishments. Then comes the day we think we know it all because we have somewhat mastered the basic guidelines. But our Teacher knows we don't get most of it because we still resort to doing things the way we did before our training.

Sometimes we want control of the recipe for our experiences. But a Master Chef knows His students will need help. I saw saving the place we named Cozy Homestead as my way to preserve our life as a family. And though we did not lose our home that day, we still faced the struggle of repairing it. In that experience God taught me to completely trust His new way and His recipe for my life.

God is beside you in your situation, and it is His power and His presence that will lead you to safety and peace.

COMFORT FOOD FOR THOUGHT
God is always with you.

Applesauce Spice Squares

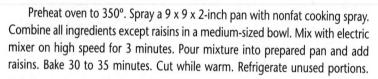

¾ cup applesauce
1½ cups flour
1 cup sugar
¼ cup water
1 teaspoon baking soda
¾ teaspoon salt
¼ teaspoon cinnamon
⅛ teaspoon ground cloves
⅛ teaspoon ground allspice
½ teaspoon baking powder
3 egg whites
¼ cup raisins

Preheat oven to 350°. Spray a 9 x 9 x 2-inch pan with nonfat cooking spray. Combine all ingredients except raisins in a medium-sized bowl. Mix with electric mixer on high speed for 3 minutes. Pour mixture into prepared pan and add raisins. Bake 30 to 35 minutes. Cut while warm. Refrigerate unused portions.

Serves: 9   Fat Grams: 1   Calories: 190

What's on Your Plate?

1. Have you been trying to save yourself, another person, or a certain way of life? Take time to sense God's presence beside you.

2. Are you frozen in certain areas of your life? What words of guidance and leading are you hearing that will allow you to move forward?

3. What fires are you putting out right now? Can you find a way to stop using a glass of water and ask God for an extinguisher?

4. Think of a time when you strongly felt God's presence. Trust that feeling. Maybe this experience will be the first time you feel He is beside you. Hold on to that truth.

5. What is God teaching you to let go of? If you are holding on because you are afraid, ask God for strength and gentle leading through this change.

God's Recipe for Patience

I waited patiently for the LORD; he turned to me and heard my cry. He lifted me out of the slimy pit, out of the mud and mire; he set my feet on a rock and gave me a firm place to stand. He put a new song in my mouth, a hymn of praise to our God. Many will see and fear and put their trust in the LORD.

PSALM 40:1-3

Be still before the LORD and wait patiently for him; do not fret when men succeed in their ways, when they carry out their wicked schemes.

PSALM 37:7

And so after waiting patiently, Abraham received what was promised.

HEBREWS 6:15

Eight

Letting Things Set
Waiting on the Lord

"Kids, this is very hard for me…I have been wrestling with the Lord about it, but I want to be obedient to God. There is something I feel God wants me to talk to you about."

Tracy's father started up a conversation out of the blue as he and I were lifting Tracy from his hospital bed to a wheelchair. Tracy could barely hold his head up as his entire body drooped left, which was his paralyzed side. We were still getting him situated when his father requested something a bit baffling for the moment and more than a little upsetting. He asked us to continue to tithe—give ten percent of our income to the church—during this time of upheaval.

"Okay," my husband said, trying to look up at his father, his fatigue apparent. This obviously was not going to be a good time for conversation, so Tracy made it simple. But his response and my father-in-law's request sent me into a tailspin of defensive thoughts. I was angered by the suggestion. We were barely making ends meet and still had a long road paved with medical bills to follow. How could anyone bring this up right now?

I tried to act calm as I interjected what I considered to be rational thought in the moment. "Tracy, I think this is something we need to pray about before we jump into giving something away we don't even have. Right now, I don't have a clue how we are going to make ends meet. I really want to pray about this before we make any quick decisions. Okay?"

"Fine," he said with finality. The last thing in the world he was concerned about right then was finances. For me—the one juggling these details—our finances had become a constant source of concern. We ended the discussion and focused on getting Tracy settled. That was the most important thing.

But my mind did not let go of the topic all day. Later I went to my parents' home so I could discuss it with my mom. Actually, I vented more than I discussed. "You are not going to believe what Dad Hall thinks we should keep on doing," I said, crying. "He thinks we should keep on tithing!" Only a mother could have possibly interpreted what I was saying between deep sobs.

"Honey, I completely agree with your father-in-law," she affirmed with gentleness. A lot of good my mother was. So I went to talk with my friend Mary Beth. "You are not going to believe what Wayne Hall and my mom think we should do. They think Tracy and I should keep on tithing. Can you believe it?" I asked, believing Mary Beth would see how ridiculous the whole idea was. She was a rational, intelligent person.

"Dawn, I completely agree," she said wholeheartedly and with compassion.

Am I the only one who hasn't lost their mind here? Hello? Can't they all see the predicament we're in? Don't they care? I drove home bawling the entire way. I look back at how raw my emotions were at the time. It was just eight days after Tracy's surgery, and I was vulnerable and scared. I believe most of all that I was lonely. I felt very alone in the circumstances. And this perceived betrayal by people I cared about multiplied the loneliness.

Exhaustion consumed me. I headed straight for the couch and fell to my knees with my face buried in my arms. It was at that point the truth hit me like a brick to the head. "Dawn, you could have a million dollars and give it all to Me, but I don't want it unless you want to give it with a gracious heart," I heard God say. It doesn't get any truer than that.

In that moment of desperation and loneliness, I was given complete peace. I knew without a shadow of a doubt we were to continue tithing. From that moment on that huge issue ceased to exist as a barrier. Tithing became a source of order and peace in a time of chaos and uncertainty. I did what I knew God wanted us to do, and I believe my faithfulness allowed me to receive God's faithfulness.

I called Tracy in the hospital that evening. I was crying again, but this time they were tears of joy. "What's wrong?" he asked with concern. I told him what I experienced and let him know I agreed that we were to continue tithing, even though I didn't know how we would do it. And, of course, that was the entire point. I was not meant to know how "we" would do it. I was to have faith in how God would do it. I was meant to wait upon the Lord's provision for myself and my family.

The next evening we received our very first two financial gifts since Tracy's diagnosis. One was from my cousin Cathy and her husband Craig, the other was from my Aunt Diane and Uncle Ronnie. I believe those gifts were affirmation from God that we were doing the right thing. And it was not a matter of reward for obedience. It seemed to be a clear lesson about trusting and believing in God's care. My loneliness and sense of betrayal were rooted in my feelings of being distant from God's love and protection. This experience reminded me that I was still in His embrace.

Releasing Our Hold

While I believe in the importance of tithing, this is not what I am sharing with you through the telling of this story. I don't know what your circumstances are. I do know that in our darkest times, when hope fades throughout the day, we can feel distance between ourselves and God. Our instinct is to hold on to everything we have as a way to protect ourselves. Just when God calls us to open our hearts to His provision, His faithfulness, and His care, we are wallowing in our worries and shutting down the part of our hearts that trusts and believes.

The tithing you are called to in this time of your life might be different than a financial offering. Maybe you already tithe. Maybe you give of your time and resources even as you face difficulties. But have you given yourself over to God and His purpose for your situation? These are the times to draw near to the Provider and Protector. Don't let false thoughts of loneliness or of being abandoned replace the truth. It is easy to run from God's love when we need it most. Either we feel we don't deserve His love or we are afraid to fully trust it because we have been let down by others or by other situations. The letting go, the opening up, the trusting…it can be painful and may trigger long-avoided emotions.

Waiting on the Lord and letting things set for a while is not easy. I don't believe there is such a thing as inactive waiting. In the silence or times of apparent inactivity or direction we are called to do very important work. We pray, actively live out patience, listen, and pay attention to our lives. Waiting on God truly can be one of the most profound spiritual times along your difficult journey.

All we have comes from the Lord. Learning to release our hold on what He entrusts to us gives us the freedom and heart to receive more from Him…and pass it along.

Sharing the Provision

I dared to ask God for a special Christmas gift. It was three days before Christmas, and the leading news story for the day was about some friends of ours. Their barn burned down and the fire killed all of their horses along with their other pets. I wanted to really help them, not just with $10 or $20, but with a bigger gift. So I prayed about it. I didn't say anything to anyone except Tracy. He also wanted to really bless them. We agreed if we received any financial gifts beyond our Christmas gift money, we'd consider it God's way to help us bless our friends. The very next day we received three surprise checks adding up to over $200. God is not only faithful in meeting all our needs, He also blesses us in our desire to bless others. It was the greatest Christmas gift of all.

COMFORT FOOD FOR THOUGHT

God is faithful.

Slow-Roasted Chicken with Herbs

1 4- to 5-pound chicken with
   all excess fat removed
2 teaspoons dried tarragon leaves
2 teaspoons dried basil
2 teaspoons parsley
2 teaspoons dried thyme
1 teaspoon garlic salt
½ teaspoon freshly ground black pepper
1 small lemon cut into quarters

Preheat oven to 375°. Remove everything from the cavity (inside) of the chicken and discard (unless you want to cook it on the side or save for later). Rinse the chicken inside and out with cold water and pat dry with paper towels. Place the chicken on a rack in a roasting pan with the breast side up. Set aside. In a small bowl, stir together the tarragon leaves, basil, parsley, thyme, garlic salt, and pepper until well mixed. Sprinkle 1 tablespoon of the mixed herbs in the cavity of the chicken, and then sprinkle the outside of the entire chicken with the remaining herbs. Put the lemon wedges inside the cavity of the chicken. Wrap the roasting pan with heavy-duty aluminum foil.

Bake for 1 hour. Lift foil and cut the band of skin or string holding the chicken legs together and remove string so the thighs will cook evenly.

Cover again with foil and continue baking at 375° for another 1¼ to 1½ hours longer. The larger the chicken, the longer it will take to cook. The chicken is done when an instant-read thermometer inserted into the thickest part of the chicken thigh reads 185°. Make sure the thermometer does not touch the bone. Roasting time depends on the weight of your chicken.

Take the chicken out of the oven and let it sit, covered, for about ten minutes. Letting it sit is called "letting the chicken rest." Doing this helps the chicken retain more juices when you cut into it.

Discard the lemon wedges. Before eating, remove the chicken skin to avoid all of that cholesterol.

Serves: 6 to 8   Fat Grams: 9   Calories: 226

What's on Your Plate?

1. How is God calling you to be faithful?

2. What are you holding on to tightly at this time? Is God asking you to release it?

3. When have you had to trust God completely? Were you able to give your situation over to Him then? What happened?

4. God longs for you to experience His faithfulness. How do you hope you will see His faithfulness manifest in your current circumstances? If His faithfulness appears in a different way, will you be able to let go of your expectations and trust Him?

5. How can you "tithe" in your life right now? What giving are you doing to make room for the receiving?

6. While you wait on the Lord, spend time in His Word so that His promises are replacing your doubts and anxieties.

God's Recipe for Giving and Receiving

But when you give to the needy, do not let your left hand know what your right hand is doing, so that your giving may be in secret. Then your Father, who sees what is done in secret, will reward you.

MATTHEW 6:3-4

So I say to you: Ask and it will be given to you; seek and you will find; knock and the door will be opened to you. For everyone who asks receives; he who seeks finds; and to him who knocks, the door will be opened.

LUKE 11:9-10

You open your hand and satisfy the desires of every living thing.

PSALM 145:16

For God did not give us a spirit of timidity, but a spirit of power, of love and of self-discipline.

2 TIMOTHY 1:7

Be joyful in hope, patient in affliction, faithful in prayer. Share with God's people who are in need. Practice hospitality.

ROMANS 12:12-13

Nine

Borrowing a Cup of Sugar
Asking for and Accepting Help

Does your mind race with questions about your circumstances? Nothing feels normal when you are caught in a whirlwind of emotional difficulties. If your concerns are physical, eventually they will manifest into emotional burdens and nonstop dialogue in your head will begin. Suddenly, life is flooded with questions.

I was so lost in thought some days that I did not even recognize how much I was struggling to complete a task that in the past would have been no big deal. When you are caught in that mode, sometimes you don't even know to ask for help. And you certainly don't know how to reach out. It is almost as if you are living a separate life in your heart and head. My head was busy worrying, planning, and forgetting while my heart was busy praying, pleading, and weeping. One big circus took place within me every day.

During my hardest times, my days started with questions and they just kept coming. *Will we make it today? Will Tracy make it through another day? How can I keep going? What is this going to do to the girls?* Neither of us knew the answers to those questions, but we knew the answer that mattered. God was in charge and He loved us.

Asking for Help

It was a gorgeous summer day, and our family was at our favorite place to be on a Sunday morning, Calvary Assembly of God in Toledo, Ohio—our home church. We had been worshiping at this awesome Bible-teaching church ever since the summer of 1987. Our weekly church service was how we recharged our spiritual batteries and reconnected with friends. Singing praise and worship songs with hundreds of other people who loved and longed for a closer relationship with God was our weekly dose of inspirational medicine that comforted our weary souls.

As was common for Tracy and me, tears flowed from our eyes as we sang praise songs. We never used to become so emotional, but ever since Tracy's cancer diagnosis our pain and gratitude rushed out of us in God's presence. At first we tried to hold our tears back, but then we realized that this wasted energy could be spent worshiping God. The simple but beautiful gift of having one another and our precious girls was all we needed to think about on Sundays.

Along with the day's delivery of tears of gratitude was an overload of heavy burdens I had been mentally, spiritually, and emotionally carrying alone for way too long.

When someone is first diagnosed with a terminal illness and is of youthful age, people are more likely to intercede on your behalf and help out. However, when you are dealing with a long-term illness and the weeks turn into months, and the months turn into years, and the years pass by, people tend to forget the day-to-day struggles a family like ours goes through just to survive. It is nobody's fault; their lives have to go on as well. But to the one facing the continued struggle, it can be a lonely experience.

In church I could ask God for the help and strength I needed. I was not good at asking people for assistance…but I had learned to turn to the Lord with my raw emotions, my pleas for help, and my tears without reservation.

One morning after our time of singing and before the sermon began, I decided to go to the restroom to wipe my face. I could just imagine streams of mascara along my cheeks. As I made my way to the bathroom I heard a friendly and familiar voice call to me.

"Hey, Dawn!" It was our good friend Jim about 20 feet behind me. He is the ultimate optimist. He is able to see beyond the circumstances of what is and see what could be. Jim is the older brother I never had, and he and his wife, Cheryl, were solid Christian mentors for Tracy and me.

I mustered up as much energy as I possibly could to deliver a cheerful "Hi!" But I wasn't fooling Mr. Optimist, whose smile hit the floor as soon as he saw my face. "How are you," I asked, trying to divert attention away from myself.

"Oh, Dawn," he said with compassion and walked toward me, reaching out his arms. I just stood there trying not to cry as big pools of tears welled up in my eyes. It was a gift to see the concerned look of a trusted confidant who cared about me. I didn't say anything. I couldn't.

In simpler times, when a neighbor came to your back door and held up a measuring cup, you could guess that they needed to borrow a cup of sugar. Of course, it was never really borrowing because the neighbor would not give that exact cup of sugar back. But you knew that some day down the road you would probably find yourself midway through mixing up ingredients for a pie or a batch of cookies and you would be just short of the amount of required sugar. This is the give-and-take of a community. And how much more are we blessed to give and take within the community of Christ.

Like a comforting father, Jim wrapped his big strong arms around me and hugged me, and my tears broke loose. God knew what I needed when I needed it. It was a time of healing and grieving.

Without asking for help...I was asking for help. Jim saw my empty cup and knew just how to fill it that day. He even came up with an idea for a fundraiser during that encounter. Such a servant. But you know, the greatest gift was his ability to see my need. I realized I had to open up to others just as I was doing to the Lord. It isn't easy to admit you can no longer plod through life alone, but this confession makes room in your life for God's abundance.

Accepting Help

I was barely making it, and it was indeed the grace of God that carried me through the darker moments. When I couldn't take any more demands and I was at the end of my rope, God would provide what we needed at the perfect time. Strangers and acquaintances, whom I lovingly refer to as "silent angels," would secretly mail us money. Friends would show up at our door out of the blue with financial gifts that would help carry us through. It was truly amazing to witness God in action through the body of Christ.

God had our family in the palm of His hand. We were totally relying on Him every day for everything. There was no self-reliance whatsoever. And with so many spiritual lessons related to letting go, this big step was about learning to receive. I cannot say which is more difficult; they both seem to go against the stubborn or determined nature many of us have developed in our lifetimes.

Goodness, part of the thrill of being an adult is that sense of independence and self-sufficiency. The catch is that many of us take independence too far. We forget that we are still God's very dependent children. When you learn to let go and move on to the lesson of learning to ask for and receive help, you cannot ever again take credit for what you have and who you are because it is all of and from God. Your identity is in Christ alone.

I pray for you as you also face these lessons. You might shake with fear or frustration when you first need to ask for help. Emotions may overwhelm you, but they will also become your salvation because they will do the asking when you are not able. One Sunday morning Jim saw the pleading in my eyes. He reached out, gave me the assurance I so desperately needed, and just like that, I learned to accept a helping hand. My life was changed forever.

COMFORT FOOD FOR THOUGHT

God gives us help through the body of Christ.

Harvest Cookies

4 egg whites
½ cup NutraSweet Spoonful
    (or ½ cup sugar)
¾ cup brown sugar
¼ cup applesauce
½ teaspoon vanilla
1 teaspoon baking soda
½ teaspoon lite salt
1 teaspoon cinnamon
½ teaspoon ground cloves or nutmeg
2 cups whole wheat flour
2 medium apples, peeled and chopped (approximately 1 cup)
½ cup chopped nuts (optional)

Preheat oven to 375°. Spray cookie sheet with nonfat spray. Beat egg whites until foamy. Mix egg whites with NutraSweet, brown sugar, applesauce, and vanilla. Stir in baking soda, salt, cinnamon, and ground cloves (or nutmeg) until well mixed. Stir in whole wheat flour, one cup at a time. Mix well. Stir in chopped apples (and nuts, if desired). Place teaspoonfuls onto cookie sheet. Bake for 5 to 6 minutes (until bottoms are golden brown).

Serves: 54 to 60   Fat Grams: .75   Calories: (with NutraSweet) 34
(with sugar) 40

What's on Your Plate?

1. When you meet God at the foot of the cross, you begin to learn how to let go, how to ask, and how to receive. Start each day with thoughts of doing all three. This lesson will become the most valuable of all.

2. Think about how great you feel when you are able to meet the needs of a friend or even a stranger. When you allow another person to help you, they receive the gift of following God's lead to care for you.

3. How are you asking for help without asking? Are there people in your life who hear this plea? If not, pray for these people to come into your life.

4. Ask yourself the question that opens up the floodgates of many more questions: "What are my needs?" If you can let yourself realize what your needs are, you are better able to communicate them with those who are able to help.

5. God's answer is love. And even when you cannot find a way to ask for it, He is the one who knows just what you need. You are His child. Rest in this identity and feel the weight of your burden lifted, day by day.

God's Recipe for Goodness

I will see the goodness of the LORD in the land of the living. Wait for the LORD; be strong and take heart and wait for the LORD.

PSALM 27:13-14

How can I repay the LORD for all his goodness to me? I will lift up the cup of salvation and call on the name of the LORD. I will fulfill my vows to the LORD in the presence of all his people.

PSALM 116:12-14

His divine power has given us everything we need for life and godliness through our knowledge of him who called us by his own glory and goodness...For this very reason, make every effort to add to your faith goodness; and to goodness, knowledge; and to knowledge, self-control; and to self-control, perseverance; and to perseverance, godliness; and to godliness, brotherly kindness; and to brotherly kindness, love. For if you possess these qualities in increasing measure, they will keep you from being ineffective and unproductive in your knowledge of our Lord Jesus Christ.

2 PETER 1:3,5-9

Ten

A Snack of Sweets
Goodness in the Midst of Pain

When we are busy putting together the heavy pieces of our lives, arranging them just so, turning them over to God, serving them up, and asking for help from others, a bit of something delectable can be very comforting. I was given a delicious surprise during a very troubling time. And like a dieter who has gone too long without a bit of chocolate and is suddenly faced with a box of truffles, I realized I was starving for sweetness.

Considering the Dessert Tray

"Dawn, you are the epitome of what we look for in a Mrs. Ohio. Would you be interested in entering our next Mrs. Ohio pageant?" This question came from the director of this pageant after one of my speaking events in Toledo.

I had visions of the pageants I had seen on television—magazine models parading up and down a runway—and I promptly replied that my body was not meant for that kind of thing. I worked hard to stay at my current size, but I could not see myself becoming pageant material.

"You are fine! We don't have a swimsuit competition. Instead, we have aerobic wear. The largest number of points comes from the interview section. Think about it. I think you'd do great."

I was flattered but not convinced enough to give it more consideration.

Nine months later I received a postcard promoting the Mrs. Ohio pageant. Again I was flattered, but I thought little of it and tossed the postcard into the office trash. Karen, my assistant, must have noticed the content of that card because she literally jumped out of her seat to retrieve the invitation.

"You have to do this, Dawn. You just have to. You'd be terrific, and it'd be good publicity for business." She threw in that last part to appeal to the practical woman in me. I watched her as she waved the postcard in her hand as if she had the winning ticket to a lottery. Karen has always been one of my biggest cheerleaders. At times I think she believes in my abilities more than I do. If she isn't patting me on the back and saying, "Good job, Dawn," then she's giving me a kick in the pants while saying, "Come on, Dawn. You can do it!"

"Let me think on it. I'll tack the postcard above the desk as a reminder, and in a couple weeks I'll decide." My response didn't totally appease her, but she knew it was all I could offer right then.

But every time I saw Karen, the same nagging question left her lips: "Are you going to enter the pageant?" And every day I gave her the same shrug of my shoulders. I had significant and valid reasons why I couldn't. But Karen had a positive response to every argument. She missed her calling to be a lawyer but obviously had heeded the call to be a very persistent friend.

One night at dinner I mentioned the pageant to Tracy and our girls. Tracy and I agreed we should pray about it. Whitney and Ashley were excited and definitely casting yes votes. Most everyone I mentioned it to thought I should go for it. People offered to pay the entrance fee and buy the gown. I was stunned by the enthusiasm and offers.

At the end of my two weeks, I explained my decision to Karen. "I won't use money my family needs, so I will strike up a deal: If God really wants me to do this pageant, then He'll have to provide the entry fee, the cost of the gown, pageant clothes, and Tracy's tuxedo. If enough money does not come in by the entrance deadline, so be it. If enough money does come in, I'll enter. Fair enough?" With that impossible list of requirements, I was pretty sure I would not be walking across a stage in heels anytime soon. But at least I was letting myself consider the dessert tray during a time when I was feasting primarily on the daily requirements of work and work, with a side of work.

The Taste of Sweetness

The next morning Karen sent letters out to the business people in Swanton. Within days we were inundated with checks and donations. Our doctor, local grocery store, and bank even sponsored me. Our dentist whitened my teeth for free. The local wedding shop offered any dress at half price. Enough sponsorship money came in from our community so that everything was paid for, including Tracy's tux and 22 tickets to the pageant to give away as thank-you gifts to the sponsors.

Selecting a gown was a family effort and a lot of fun. I'll never forget the looks on Tracy's, Whitney's, and Ashley's faces as I walked out of the dressing room for the first time wearing a gown.

Their jaws dropped in unison as their eyes gazed at the sparkling sequins covering the white-on-white fitted bodice and princess neckline ballroom gown. Layers of soft sheer chiffon flowed from my waistline down to the floor. I walked toward my family and felt like an angel.

With the love and support of my family and a community behind me, I headed into the pageant with no idea what to expect. My fears were put to rest when I was greeted with kindness and offers from other contestants to teach me pageant basics, such as how to walk, perform the dance steps, and prepare for the interview and other portions of the program.

The night before the actual pageant I shared a room with a woman from Sidney, Ohio. She was a pro at this. Late at night I looked across the room at her, envious that she was able to sleep peacefully while I counted sheep. I was a bag of nerves and could just imagine the bags that would be under my eyes in the morning.

Finally the pageant began. The curtain rose and the dazzling opening number was performed. I could not stop smiling—not out of fear or lack of sleep as I had imagined—but out of pure joy. I was tasting the sweetness of this adventure. Throughout the evening I had moments of poise and moments of near disaster. At one point I was completely in the wrong place at the wrong time and starting to change into the wrong outfit. I have to laugh when I recall running frantically up the stairs, around corners, and along the back stage to make it just in time to go forward and present my platform speech. And while I was a bit disappointed with my performance, I quickly reminded myself to savor every bit of this experience: the female camaraderie, the celebration of womanhood and marriage, the luxury of spending time and energy on myself. The entire time I thought about how special I was in

God's eyes. He sees me as a woman dressed in a white gown. He places me in His hand, holds me, and calls me His daughter. Oh, how that is easy to forget when life is difficult.

The Escort of My Dreams

The evening gown segment was by far my favorite part of the pageant. Each contestant walked down a beautiful staircase and met her husband waiting at the foot of the steps. Days before the pageant began, I asked Tracy to sit in his wheelchair while we were on stage together. "It'll ease my concern of you falling," I said. "I can meet you at the foot of the stairs just like all the other couples, but I'll just walk next to you in your wheelchair across stage."

"No way. I know I can make it across the stage using my walker without falling. Dawn, you have to let me do this." He was adamant. Cancer had robbed him of too many pleasures in life already. He wasn't going to allow this disease to steal this moment from him, from us.

Just as he was determined to do, Tracy met me at the foot of the stairs *standing*, holding firm to his walker with both hands. His face, belly, feet, and hands were swollen from the steroids and countless medications he was on…and he was handsome. It took a lot of courage to stand in front of a full house. I was so proud of him. We gave each other a sweet kiss. So much love and understanding was in that one embrace.

The highlight of the pageant for us was when Tracy and I received the only standing ovation of the evening, which came after I was announced the winner of the Mrs. Ohio Community Service Award for 2000. The crowd went nuts with applause and cheers. The people we knew who came to support us were the loudest cheerleaders. I looked at my precious Grandma Schaefer, who was dabbing away her tears. I thought of how Tracy's father was waiting with the wheelchair backstage and showing tremendous support to both of us.

The entire evening and the steps it took to reach that stage were all part of one big comforting hug. I felt embraced by God's goodness. And yes, it was oh so sweet.

COMFORT FOOD FOR THOUGHT
God is good.

Spicy Raisin Cookies

1 cup apple butter
    (use your favorite brand)
1 cup dark brown sugar
½ cup NutraSweet Spoonful
    (or ½ cup sugar)
6 egg whites
1 teaspoon vanilla
1 teaspoon baking soda
1 teaspoon lite salt
1 teaspoon cinnamon
½ teaspoon ground cloves
2 cups whole wheat flour
1 cup self-rising flour
2 cups raisins
⅓ cup chopped pecans

Preheat oven to 375°. Spray a cookie sheet with nonfat cooking spray. Beat the first nine ingredients together with mixer at medium speed until well blended. Add both kinds of flour, one cup at a time, and then by hand stir in raisins and pecans. Drop by teaspoonful onto prepared cookie sheet. Bake for 7 minutes.

Glaze:
½ cup dark brown sugar
½ cup fat-free cream cheese (I prefer Healthy Choice)
1 teaspoon vanilla

Blend well. Quickly put a thin layer of glaze on cookies while they are still warm.

Serves: 72   Fat Grams: .4   Calories: (with NutraSweet) 47
(with sugar) 52

What's on Your Plate?

1. What bit of sweetness is God offering you?

2. When you think about taking care of or pampering yourself, what comes to mind? Follow through with one of those ideas.

3. Imagine yourself being cared for by God. Reflect on how special you are to the One who made you.

4. Is there something you have been saying no to because it seems selfish? Revisit whatever that might be...and consider doing it.

5. Plan a date for yourself. You can bring a friend or loved one or just go by yourself. Have your hair done and go out to eat. Go for coffee and wander through a bookstore. Walk downtown and window-shop. Turn off the phone, take a long bath, and then watch a favorite movie in your pajamas. The possibilities are endless.

6. If you journal, record times of sweetness you are experiencing even in the midst of hard times. These will help give you courage as you continue and will remind you to savor their goodness.

God's Recipe for Abundance

You crown the year with your bounty, and your carts overflow with abundance. The grasslands of the desert overflow; the hills are clothed with gladness. The meadows are covered with flocks and the valleys are mantled with grain; they shout for joy and sing.

PSALM 65:11-13

You gave abundant showers, O God; you refreshed your weary inheritance. Your people settled in it, and from your bounty, O God, you provided for the poor.

PSALM 68:9-10

They feast on the abundance of your house; you give them drink from your river of delights. For with you is the fountain of life; in your light we see light.

PSALM 36:8-9

You will pray to him, and he will hear you, and you will fulfill your vows.

JOB 22:27

The ordinances of the LORD are sure and altogether righteous. They are more precious than gold, than much pure gold; they are sweeter than honey, than honey from the comb.

PSALM 19:9-10

Eleven

Icing on the Cake
God's Extra-Special Touch

"Think about it! I have a white gown for the pageant. You'll have your tux until the Monday after the pageant. It's our sixteenth wedding anniversary that week. We always wanted to renew our vows. Right?" I asked.

Tracy was giving me his full attention. He knew my brainstorming hat was securely on and there was no avoiding me.

The details for the Mrs. Ohio pageant were all coming together so perfectly. It seemed as though it was truly orchestrated by God's hand. And as I considered how thankful I was for the opportunity to do something so fun and out of the ordinary, I became more grateful for Tracy's love and the life we shared. And, well, when I tried on that white beautiful gown, thoughts of our wedding and marriage flooded my mind. If we renewed our vows it would be a way to make this special event even more memorable and personally significant.

I continued as Tracy tried to keep up with my leapfrogging thoughts. "The day after the pageant is Sunday, so why don't we renew our vows after church? The girls can stand with us. I'm sure Pastor Tom would not mind doing a little ceremony for us after the service. What do you think?"

Tracy lit up like a little kid at a candy store. He was every bit as excited about the possibility as I was. It was something we had wanted to do for our fifteenth anniversary the previous year, but we hadn't due to finances.

I made some calls and discovered that several kind people at the church had been discussing doing something to celebrate our life and our marriage. And this expression of love was from a church we had been attending for a short time. Once again, God was going before us, working out the details and showing us His tender love and faithfulness with each step.

My friend Lisa was not only encouraging but immediately had fabulous ideas about decorating the fellowship hall, recruiting helpers, finding a caterer, and the list went on and on. Her enthusiasm made me feel so good.

Before I knew it, the big day of the pageant was followed by the even bigger day of our vow renewals. I must say, with all the kindness and creativity lavished on us by the good folks of Waterville Open Bible Church, this wedding and reception turned out even nicer than our first. It was a gift of a lifetime.

I wonder how God will offer you icing on the cake. I imagine it will come when you least expect it and when you need it most. This weekend was so unexpected. I was looking at life through a lens of brokenness in many ways. Tracy was under hospice care, which is typically assigned when one has less than six months to live. I tried very hard to savor my time with him. I noticed how loving he was when we spoke about our life and our girls. I paid attention to his words and how he viewed faith and God's purpose. But even as I tried to see life's many textures and wonders, I was not expecting to see a time of such joy.

God performs miracles daily. Sometimes we stop to notice them and other times we rush on by them. But every once in awhile, God plants one right in the middle of your hurried path. It is too tall to climb over and too wide to step around on your way to taking care of life's business. All you can do is stop, fall to your knees, and praise Him.

Maybe you are still trying to step around something that is meant for goodness. I know how hard it is to take a break from worry. We seem to want to take it along with us wherever we go. A feeling of security comes from whatever becomes our usual way of doing things. So when a celebration presents itself or you have a chance to go out wearing your prettiest dress without the cloak of worry…let yourself experience God's extra-special something.

I am so thankful I accepted the gifts of the pageant and the renewing of our wedding vows. I had to step right over guilt to reach these celebrations of life, but I did it. And those "something specials" became two of the most precious memories I have. Tracy and I honored more than our vows in the beauty of our church's sanctuary. We honored a lifetime together in those 16 years of marriage. We celebrated a precious family and two incredible little girls. We even rejoiced in a time of struggle that was drawing us closer to one another. The weekend gave us a taste of sweetness; this celebration of our love and God's abundance was icing on the cake.

Comfort Food for Thought
God offers abundant life.

Peach Spice Cake

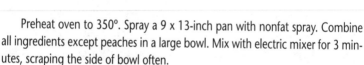

1½ cups applesauce
3 cups wheat flour
1 cup sugar
1 cup brown sugar
½ cup water
2 teaspoons baking soda
1½ teaspoons lite salt
½ teaspoon cinnamon
½ teaspoon ground cloves
¼ teaspoon ground allspice
1 teaspoon baking powder
6 egg whites
1 29-ounce can sliced peaches, drained

Preheat oven to 350°. Spray a 9 x 13-inch pan with nonfat spray. Combine all ingredients except peaches in a large bowl. Mix with electric mixer for 3 minutes, scraping the side of bowl often.

Pour mixture into prepared pan. Arrange sliced peaches on top of batter, pressing each peach slice down so that top of each slice shows and ¼ of the peach slice is in batter. Bake 37 to 47 minutes or until knife inserted in middle comes out clean. Cut while warm.

Spicy whipped topping:
2 packages Dream Whip
1 teaspoon cinnamon
½ teaspoon allspice

Prepare Dream Whip according to directions on the package, and then blend cinnamon and allspice into topping and spoon onto cake. Refrigerate unused portions.

Serves: 24   Fat Grams: 2   Calories: 130

What's on Your Plate?

1. God has far greater blessings in store for you than you have ever thought of, dreamed of, or imagined. You might be ready to hold on to that truth right now. If so, grab it with both hands and your heart. If the idea of blessing seems far from your circumstances right now, ask God to give you a spirit of hope.

2. What is something you can celebrate during this time? Is a rite of passage taking place in your family? Or has someone reached a milestone? Have you accomplished something you never thought possible? Take time for the celebrations because they too are a part of this time of your life.

3. In what ways do you show your love for others?

4. How has someone blessed you with a surprise? Think on that time and consider how God's blessing can be so much greater. If that person is still in your life, thank them for creating that special memory for you.

5. Plan a day to make or buy some unfrosted cupcakes. Invite some friends over for an "icing on the cake" day. As you spread on the chocolate, the sprinkles, the swirls of sweetness, let it be a time to rejoice in God's goodness, His promises, and the abundance He brings to your life.

God's Recipe for Transformation and Forgiveness

In him we have redemption through his blood, the forgiveness of sins, in accordance with the riches of God's grace that he lavished on us with all wisdom and understanding.

EPHESIANS 1:7-8

Bear with each other and forgive whatever grievances you may have against one another. Forgive as the Lord forgave you. And over all these virtues put on love, which binds them all together in perfect unity.

COLOSSIANS 3:13-14

Create in me a pure heart, O God, and renew a steadfast spirit within me.

PSALM 51:10

Blessed are they whose transgressions are forgiven, whose sins are covered. Blessed is the man whose sin the Lord will never count against him.

ROMANS 4:7-8

They will celebrate your abundant goodness and joyfully sing of your righteousness. The LORD is gracious and compassionate, slow to anger and rich in love.

PSALM 145:7-8

Twelve

Finger Food
Little Things Do Matter

The sounds of little girls scurrying about in the kitchen awakened me one Saturday morning when Tracy and I were both enjoying a rare day to sleep in. While scrunching my eyes closed, I imagined the best possible scenario attached to those noises... maybe Whitney and Ashley were surprising me by cleaning. A moment later many other images started to push away this one good thought. I saw messes. I saw misuse of electrical appliances. I saw more work for me later if I feigned sleep for another minute.

I approached the kitchen like a cop on a bust...slow, easy steps so I would not give the would-be criminals any warning of my entrance. By the time I reached the room the crime was well under way. One daughter focused seriously on the concoction she was vigorously stirring in a huge bowl. The other child was standing on top of the counter next to the kitchen sink searching fearlessly for the secret ingredient needed to make their next amazing creation.

My girls had chosen to experiment at a time when money was tight...and to me, food was money. The scene looked like a big stash of cash headed for the garbage.

"Girls," I said in a very calm, flat voice, "what are you doing?"

"We're creating, Mommy!" Their little voices rang out in unison. Faces radiating happiness and enthusiasm reflected their pride in helping their mommy.

"*What* are you creating?"

"We haven't given it a name yet," one of the girls said.

"Well," I asked hesitantly, "what's in it?"

"Peanut butter, tuna, and pineapple so far."

I felt my Adam's apple slide down my throat. I bit my tongue. Giving them the benefit of the doubt, but knowing full well it was going to taste terrible, I walked over and smelled it first. I kept my thoughts to myself and gave them my lips-pressed-together grin.

"Taste it, Mommy, taste it!"

Okay, a mother's love has limits. I thought it was unconditional, but this was a test of a new level. I faked taking a nibble. That charade, however, required me to smell the concoction up close and personal. My stomach turned.

"It's not good, is it, Mom." My acting was not fooling anyone.

I didn't want to pour salt in their wounds, but it didn't matter how long they looked in our cupboards, there was nothing that could have been added to make their creation taste good. "Now girls, I appreciate your help trying to create a recipe, but you have ruined a lot of food here today." I motioned around at the bowls and utensils sitting on the counter among even more ruined ingredients. "I don't ever want you trying to cook something new unless I am with you. Okay? You guys have wasted a lot of money in food."

Instantly their faces drooped. They looked so disappointed with my response. Surely it was not the enthusiasm and appreciation they had anticipated.

"But, Mom…you do it." Many times over the years the girls had seen me throw an unsuccessful recipe into the garbage because it tasted so bad. I understood how fortunate I was that a cooking cop had not looked at me with disappointment and judgment all those times. Just think where I would be today? I might have quit trying to create the recipes God wanted to use in amazing ways later.

These small realizations are mighty in the life of a Christian. When you understand how God treats us with such loving guidance and forgiveness, you have a way to measure your own responses to others. The little things matter in big ways because the little things reflect the heart and desires of another. And while my two sweet girls were throwing away a week's worth of grocery money, their hearts were overflowing with the riches of love, joy, and care. They were trying hard to follow in my footsteps and please me. My throat tightened again, but this time with the ache of happiness.

I laughed and shook my head. "Come on, my daughters. I'll help you clean it up."

Releasing the little things that bother us during the harder times in life is not easy. In fact, we can cling to those little burdens because somehow we have a bit of control over them, and let's face it, that feels pretty good. But the sooner we learn to let go of the little nuisances and find the good in them, the sooner we can release the bigger problems to God so He can make something good from them.

Some days nothing went right for me. Eventually I understood that those ridiculous days of trouble after trouble were created by my fixation on small things gone wrong. I think I actually started to look for problems in any given situation while on my way to saying, "Oh, everything is fine." My actions and my heart had not quite caught up to my words. When I could truly give God my burdens and mistakes, big or small, I learned of a forgiveness and healing far greater than any trial. With each mess I handed to my heavenly Father, I could hear Him say, "Come on, my daughter. I'll help you clean it up."

COMFORT FOOD FOR THOUGHT
God transforms little problems into big joys.

Sweet-and-Salty Finger Food

3 cups Special K cereal
    (with dried strawberries)
¼ cup sliced almonds
¼ cup dried cranberries
¼ cup dried blueberries
dash or two of lite salt (optional)

Put all ingredients in a plastic bag. Toss gently until well mixed.

Servings: 5   Fat Grams: 3   Calories: 156

This is a healthy source of carbohydrates and proteins with a limited amount of healthy fats. Keep a plastic bag or container full of this mix in the glove compartment of your vehicle for a between-meals pick-me-up.

What's on Your Plate?

1. What little things are bringing you down lately? Which ones can you give to God right now?

2. Think of giving your problem over to His hands. Think about that each day until you truly believe it.

3. Has something small or unimportant come between you and another person? Pray for that barrier to be removed and know that you might be the one called to remove it.

4. How has a nuisance turned into a joy in your life? Are you able to laugh about something silly you or another person has done? Letting go of trivial things is a big step toward healing.

5. Look around at a mess you have made. Chances are that you have wasted a lot of your energy, time, and ability on this disaster. Let that go too. Better to stop dwelling on that right now than spend a day of worry, guilt, and regret when you could be receiving comfort, moving on, and praising God.

God's Recipe for Peace

But the wisdom that comes from heaven is first of all pure; then peace-loving, considerate, submissive, full of mercy and good fruit, impartial and sincere. Peacemakers who sow in peace raise a harvest of righteousness.

JAMES 3:17-18

Submit to God and be at peace with him; in this way prosperity will come to you. Accept instruction from his mouth and lay up his words in your heart.

JOB 22:21-22

I will lie down and sleep in peace, for you alone, O LORD, make me dwell in safety.

PSALM 4:8

Do not be anxious about anything, but in everything, by prayer and petition, with thanksgiving, present your requests to God. And the peace of God, which transcends all understanding, will guard your hearts and your minds in Christ Jesus.

PHILIPPIANS 4:6-7

Now may the Lord of peace himself give you peace at all times and in every way. The Lord be with all of you.

2 THESSALONIANS 3:16

Thirteen

The Pot Is Boiling Over
When You Feel Overwhelmed

From the day I found out about Tracy's cancer, exhaustion was a constant reality. About a year and a half after the diagnosis I was so exhausted that right after I helped the children off to school I told Tracy, "I'm just going to lie down for a little bit." I slept nonstop until Whitney and Ashley came home from school at 4:00. I couldn't believe I had slept so long...and I was still tired. I craved sleep. Within an hour I was headed back to bed for a "nap" while Tracy helped the girls with their homework. That nap lasted 14 hours.

There were many ways that cancer overwhelmed parts of our lives. Fatigue settled into all of our bones. The presence of the illness was like an unexpected houseguest who did not understand the rules of proper etiquette. It stayed way too long. It used our energy and resources and asked for more without batting an eye. It pestered us with daily demands that began to override those things that used to be important to us, such as rest, joy, and intimacy.

The Loss of Intimacy

Before Tracy's illness physical intimacy was a way for us to share our love for each other. It was also sometimes a way to release stress. But the devastating sexual side effects of brain cancer affected Tracy's self-esteem and psyche and our sex life stopped. The loss of this intimacy took its toll on me physically and psychologically. I missed giving and receiving the comfort of touch.

I'll never forget the first time I went out of my way to look sexy for him after the onset of his illness. My heart fell when he didn't even notice me. I couldn't be upset...not with Tracy anyway. But the sadness deepened as days, months, and years went by. To deal with my feelings of anger and neglect, I kept telling myself that a lot of people struggle with this in great ways and still maintain a healthy, loving relationship.

I knew I had to guard this area of my life carefully because I had heard many stories of others who divorced because of the stress of illnesses. I did not want to do anything to jeopardize our marriage. For better or for worse meant for better or for worse. I was committed to the long haul, but I needed help to get through the "for worse" part. Losing intimate relationship with Tracy was not just a physical loss, but an emotional and spiritual one as well. Lovemaking is a very important time of spiritual connection between a husband and wife. Mourning the loss of the relationship as it used to be added to my sense of being overwhelmed. My emotions seemed out of control at times.

Crying spells became part of my daily routine. I would take showers so I could cry under the running water without Tracy or the girls hearing me. I don't know if the frequent bathing or the eye drops really were hiding the fact that my heart was breaking, but I kept up that charade for quite some time.

Usually I sensed the onset of tears coming and would quickly dismiss myself from a social gathering or the dinner table. However, at times emotional distress would overwhelm me and without warning I'd have a meltdown complete with cries that came from deep within my soul. Gratefully, these occurred mostly when I was by myself in my car at a stop light or between destinations. I sat and bawled in more than a few parking lots.

My crying became a form of communication with God. I know He understands my feelings even when I don't. He is the only one who hears my silent screams and my muffled cries. He offers me comfort as I crumple at His feet. When tears betray your strong front, be sure that you let them fall. Give yourself time to feel the pain and give your pain time to seek out God's balm. You might not know what to ask for specifically, but I really believe that through the Holy Spirit our needs are heard and tended to by our heavenly Father.

Filling the Void

Food was my source of comfort and relaxation, as it had been so many times in my life. I jokingly tell people there is nothing a hot fudge brownie can't make feel better. But it wouldn't be so funny if I said there is nothing a double martini can't remedy. Food is an accepted addiction in America. Gluttony is an acceptable sin in the Christian community. Oh, the hidden struggles I had (and sometimes still do have) within myself. I was writing low-fat cookbooks and struggling with my weight. Food was the pleasure I could enjoy that did not take energy and instantly gave me a sense of comfort. Just as an alcoholic uses alcohol for all the wrong reasons, I used food for reasons other than nutritional value and suppressing hunger. Even to this day I am a recovering food addict who struggles on a daily basis.

When I am stressed I find myself reaching for whatever sounds good from the cupboard or the refrigerator. Then, somewhere between the first bite and the empty container, I become oblivious to the amount I am devouring. Before I know it, whatever package I am eating out of is empty, and I become aware that I have once again binged. Feelings of guilt, shame, and remorse fuel the need for comfort. I can lie to myself that everything is okay by suppressing my feelings with food.

When we experience loss of any kind, we are quick to fill the empty spaces in our hearts, our minds, our spirits with something...anything. We can lose a dream, a goal, a friend, a job, and the void becomes a source of sadness, anger, or frustration. Of course we want to fill it with something of comfort. I encourage you to understand your void. Get a feel for what is missing and seek out God's peace.

Those times when I cried and cried in the shower, I knew my circumstances were difficult and I obviously knew I was sad about Tracy's illness, but it took me awhile to understand that I was lonely. But God was aware of the shape of the hole in my heart and His love filled it. He surrounded me with caring people. He directed me toward writing the cookbooks, which in turn connected me with people I could minister to and be ministered by. His love soothed my restless spirit when I felt I had no one to turn to. I wanted to hide my grief from my girls and often from Tracy, but I could bare my soul to the Creator of my soul.

Prayer does not always replace my urge for chocolate or a bag of chips...but it does fill the shape of any missing piece with His everlasting peace.

COMFORT FOOD FOR THOUGHT

God's peace passes all understanding.

Carrot and Lentil Soup

1 pound lentils

8 cups water

4 cups sliced carrots

1 medium onion, finely chopped

1 46-ounce can V-8 Juice

1 28-ounce can crushed tomatoes, concentrated

1 teaspoon Liquid Smoke Hickory Seasoning

   (found in barbecue sauce section of your grocery store)

2 bay leaves

1 tablespoon plus 1 teaspoon garlic salt

2 teaspoons NutraSweet Spoonful (or 1½ tablespoons sugar)

   In a large saucepan, bring lentils and water to a rapid boil; boil for 2 minutes. Reduce heat to a simmer. Add remaining ingredients. Cover and simmer for at least two hours (until carrots and lentils are tender). Stir occasionally. Take out bay leaves before serving.

   Serves: 19   Fat Grams: .61   Calories: (with Nutrasweet) 121
                                              (with sugar) 123

What's on Your Plate?

1. How are you trying to fill a void right now? Are you making a healthy choice, or is it working against you in other ways?

2. Identify the void and ask God to fill it with His peace.

3. When you are overwhelmed, spend focused time in prayer. And on days when everything inside of you says you are too busy to pray…pray extra long.

4. How is God offering you lifelines to help you across the chasm of loss or grief or change?

5. How have you responded to your boiling point in the past? Is your experience teaching you a new way to ease the pressure of life?

God's Recipe for Joy

You have made known to me the path of life; you will fill me with joy in your presence.

PSALM 16:11

May the God of hope fill you with all joy and peace as you trust in him, so that you may overflow with hope by the power of the Holy Spirit.

ROMANS 15:13

Convinced of this, I know that I will remain, and I will continue with all of you for your progress and joy in the faith, so that through my being with you again your joy in Christ Jesus will overflow on account of me.

PHILIPPIANS 1:25-26

You will go out in joy and be led forth in peace; the mountains and hills will burst into song before you, and all the trees of the field will clap their hands.

ISAIAH 55:12

He prays to God and finds favor with him, he sees God's face and shouts for joy; he is restored by God to his righteous state.

JOB 33:26

Restore to me the joy of your salvation and grant me a willing spirit, to sustain me.

PSALM 51:12

Fourteen

Licking the Spoon
Allowing Joy into Your Life

When a heart is full of sadness, its fragility makes us vulnerable to any strong emotion. Soon we learn to guard ourselves from anything that might shake and shatter it. Even strong joy and laughter can feel painful or wrong. Sadly, in hard times we often feel guilty if we experience the taste of fun, rest, or any experience not directly related to the source of pain. A burst of laughter seems a disloyal act, though it is our heart and soul healing. Joy is God's medicine. It should not be met with shame or interpreted as being contrary to the significance of our sorrow.

Earlier I admitted how guilty I felt when I left work one afternoon so I could take a nap. Guilt snuck in many other times. But, I am happy to say, so did joy. God was going to have us lick the spoon and taste a bit of heaven's sweetness whether we were open to it or not.

One day I found myself pulling up to a drive-through to treat the girls to a Happy Meal. You wouldn't believe (or maybe you would) how much guilt and joy I felt that day. One second I would think, *How dare we spend money for Happy Meals when we owe so much for medical bills?* And the next moment I would think, *This is such a treat. This is important.* This simple exercise was not a matter of right and wrong or black and white. It was going through a drive-through, for crying out loud. When we place an activity or thought into either the right or the wrong column, we think we are simplifying life, but really we are confusing ourselves about our emotions. If we equate sadness as bad, we write off experiencing our sorrow in a way that can help lead to healing. If we consider happiness during a sad time inappropriate or inconsiderate, then we are not allowing God's Spirit of joy to enter our lives in a way that breathes hope and vitality into our journey.

It took me awhile to learn this lesson, but I finally risked breaking my heart and opened up my mouth and my soul to laugh fully, deeply, and desperately. I needed it so much. No surprise, my first rounds of laughter led to tears because joy and pain share a certain intensity. Often they intermingle as we sort out our feelings. One of the best examples of this wild ride of emotions is in the movie *Steel Magnolias*. Sally Field's character has just buried her daughter, and the rage she expresses is powerful and wild. It is followed by tears, and then bits of happier sentiments appear between her rounds of rage. She thinks of how precious her daughter was, how beautiful her grandson is, and she looks in a mirror and her reflection reminds her that the daughter she just buried thought her hair looked like a football helmet and she laughs. Then she cries.

So the roller coaster continues. This is what it is like to be on the ride of loss or regret or illness or sorrow. You cannot get off at any point, and the emotions just need to be experienced, tasted, and felt. I believe each and every emotion you feel leads you to God's comforting presence, if you let it.

Good Humor, Good Medicine

Tracy and I tried to find the humor in things as much as possible. Perhaps it was because we had always enjoyed teasing one another, but a bigger motivation was to surround the girls with the comforting joy of God's love. It needed to be visible to them so they could understand our lives were rich with many emotions and feelings. As a family we rented comedies from the library, we checked out humorous books from our cancer support group, we told and retold stories about ourselves that either were embarrassing, silly, or just plain fun. Once one of us started with "remember when..." we could sit and talk and laugh for hours. As crazy as it sounds, humor kept us from going crazy. It was one good thing we could share together. Tracy and I would spend evenings together sharing stories. It reaffirmed our commitment to one another, and even if we told the same stories over and over, the joy was fresh. We held on to that tightly because each smile, shake of the head, or giggle meant we had room in our hearts for goodness and faith.

"Remember when you were pregnant with Whitney and getting an ultrasound?" he asked me one night as we lay facing each other on our bed. We both smiled. He knew I remembered. Then he spoke in the funny mocking voice he used when he was pretending to be me. "'I knew this baby was a boy!' The nurse asked how and you said, 'I just had a feeling the baby was a boy, and now I know because I can see his little testicles on the ultrasound screen.' The nurse laughed and told you, 'Those two little spots are kidneys!'" This probably happens to lots of couples during the first ultrasound, but we just thought it was hysterical. Tracy especially brought this story up as one of my unintentionally comedic moments.

"Hey," I said, joining in the fun. "Remember when we had that surprise graduation party for Kim? I told her we were having a costume party, but really it was a surprise party for her. Her husband came as Cher and Kim was Sonny Bono. And they were the only ones dressed up!"

We both moved from reclining on our side to lying on our backs with one arm behind our heads. We allowed happy memories to linger as we savored every moment of fun we could remember. As I turned to look over at him I could see the mental wheels spinning as he scanned our life looking for another funny story to reminisce about. One after another we took turns offering happiness to the other. God blessed us with these times of intimacy during the cancer journey. Shared stories…shared joy… shared lives.

Holding Tightly to Joy

Once you allow yourself to feel joy, you are more apt to experience it. Laugh out loud at the bizarre places in which you finally find your keys each day. Watch a silly movie that would have bored you before but now can offer a happy escape. Listen to the fun things that come from the mouths of your children. Watch a sunrise or sunset from your porch or your roof, and enjoy the view.

In your time of trial, you will discover that the pieces of joy you hold on to are not always accepted, encouraged, or even noticed by others. That is when you have to cling to joy no matter what. The moment could be orchestrated by God to meet a need you have right then. If nobody else honors that bit of hope, it doesn't matter. It is yours to embrace and accept as a gift.

During one of Tracy's lengthy hospital stays, numerous doctors came in to analyze him. My husband's frustration grew each time he was asked again to try physical movements on his paralyzed side. Over and over his attempts were unsuccessful. As usual he didn't complain, but the look in his eyes told me he was discouraged.

His mother was sitting next to me at the foot of his hospital bed while yet another doctor evaluated him. All of a sudden his mother took her thumbnail and ran it firmly against the bottom of Tracy's left foot. His big toe moved for the first time in ten days. We all just stared at each other in total amazement.

"Tracy, your toe moved! Your toe moved!" his mother shouted with joy.

"Oh my gosh!" I gasped as tears of happiness ran down my face. It was the most excitement—good excitement—we had tasted in a long time.

"Did you see that, Doctor? Did you see that?" Tracy asked with astonishment. We were all in a state of shock and glee. We could hardly contain our joy and almost didn't notice the look of conflict on our doctor's face.

"Now, Mr. and Mrs. Hall," the doctor said, trying to bring us back to reality, "that was just a neurological reflex. There's nothing to get excited about."

I felt as though we were children being told to settle down, as if our excitement was not valid or appropriate. I looked up at the doctor from my chair and stood up, so to speak, for our faith and joy. "We know it is only a neurological reflex, but we haven't had a neurological reflex in ten days. We'll get excited if we want to get excited." I might have even glared at this moment.

The doctor was speechless and a bit taken aback. I hadn't meant to come across as rude, but I just couldn't let him or anyone else rob us of that moment and movement of hope. If Tracy's toe moved once, it might move again in the future. That was a spark of happiness. Tracy tried to intentionally move it. Nothing. We didn't care. We said "I love you" to each other and held on to our joy.

COMFORT FOOD FOR THOUGHT
God wants you to experience joys big or small.

Chocolate Cookies

16 egg whites
1 tablespoon plus 1 teaspoon
    baking powder
1 teaspoon lite salt
⅓ cup applesauce
⅓ cup lite corn syrup
1 tablespoon plus 1 teaspoon vanilla
2½ cups flour
1½ cups sugar and ½ cup NutraSweet Spoonful
    (or 2 cups sugar)
4 cups quick-cooking oats
1⅓ cups cocoa

Preheat oven to 375°. Spray a cookie sheet with nonfat cooking spray. Beat egg whites with baking powder, salt, applesauce, corn syrup, and vanilla until bubbly and lightly foamy. Add remaining dry ingredients. Mix well.

Drop by teaspoonfuls onto prepared cookie sheet. Bake for 9 minutes. Remove cookies from cookie sheet immediately. When cool, store in an airtight container.

Serves: 96   Fat Grams: 1.2   Calories: (with sugar and NutraSweet) 56
(with sugar only) 60

What's on Your Plate?

1. Have there been times in your life when you felt your joy was being robbed from you?

2. Think on something that made you smile recently. Let the thought bring a smile to your face even as you are troubled or busy. Consider it your joy break.

3. Ask God to change your attitude so that you can notice and receive more joy.

4. If holding on to joy seems difficult, call a friend who encourages your heart and reminds you of happy times and silly moments.

5. Dwell on Scripture that fills your perspective with gladness and hope.

6. The next time someone wants to rain on your parade, think of yourself stepping beneath the coverage of God's joy. It will protect you from the hurtful words of the faithless.

God's Recipe for Comfort

Remember your word to your servant, for you have given me hope. My comfort in my suffering is this: Your promise preserves my life.

PSALM 119:49-50

May your unfailing love be my comfort, according to your promise to your servant. Let your compassion come to me that I may live, for your law is my delight.

PSALM 119:76-77

I will turn their mourning into gladness; I will give them comfort and joy instead of sorrow.

JEREMIAH 31:13

As a mother comforts her child, so will I comfort you; and you will be comforted over Jerusalem.

ISAIAH 66:13

Fifteen

When Chicken Soup Is Not Enough
Seeking Comfort in the Grief

There is a desire for order within us that I believe helps us seek out God's order and plan for our lives. Yet this desire for order can rub against the chaos we call real life. If we spend time in one trial, so be it, but rest assured that we are quickly planning how that new path will take shape and manifest into something good. We want to bring order to our difficulties so they feel manageable and under our control.

I had tried to do this very thing. Tracy's cancer was no longer detected, and I could clearly see how this path was unfolding. In my time of gratitude I was trying to put the past six years into boxes labeled "Life with Cancer" and "Battling Death." I wanted to wrap them with tape, wire, and chains and file these experiences away.

We had endured the storm. Now we would have an amazing testimony about loving each other more deeply, growing in our faith, and trusting the Lord no matter where this path took us as a family. We would be able to speak of God's goodness through the journey of cancer survival. I saw the order of things and could feel myself breathing more easily at night, knowing what our calling was becoming. I could see how God was using the struggles in those two boxes for His glory and the hope of others.

This peace in my soul would not last long. Questions, chaos, and disturbing anger churned again when events turned in our lives.

When the Story Takes a Turn

Tracy was not feeling well. As had been his pattern recently, he started his day by throwing up, getting cleaned up and dressed for the day, reading his Bible in his recliner, and eating barely any breakfast. These simple morning tasks took him at least two or three hours. That amount of labor for such a simple morning would have frustrated him so much before, but now we had the hope of beating the cancer for good and could see this struggle as his down time for further healing. During this time Tracy said that if life continued to be so difficult and painful, he would welcome death. Yet we both saw the order of this story and were eager to see it through to healing.

On a regular day in May Tracy agreed to deliver a gift I had prepared for our teenage neighbor Jimmy, who had broken multiple fingers a few days prior. At about 11:00 my husband slowly made his way over to our young neighbor's house. While Tracy enjoyed a friendly chat with Jimmy and his dad, Ken, out on their back patio, Ken noticed Tracy's eyes start to roll back into his head. Before they knew it, Tracy was falling straight back onto the cement.

Immediately Jimmy came running over to our home screaming my name. "Dawn! Dawn!" I jumped up and met him before he made it to the door.

"Tracy fell!" he said in a panic.

Out the door I ran with Jimmy by my side. I could see Tracy lying there, unconscious, with the sun beaming down on him. Ken knelt down by Tracy's left side trying to talk with him, but there with no response.

"Oh, dear God!" I don't even recall taking steps toward Tracy. All of a sudden I was kneeling next to his right side with my right hand cupped under his head, trying desperately to awaken my husband.

"Tracy! This is Dawn. Can you hear me? Tracy, please, sweetheart, if you can hear me, please say something!" I pleaded. No reply. By now it is all I can do to remain calm and not cry. I had to maintain composure. The last thing I wanted Tracy to think (if he could hear me) was that something was wrong.

"What? What happened?" he quietly responded with closed eyes. Finally, a response. Praise God.

"Honey, you had a fall, but everything is going to be all right. Can you open your eyes?" I asked. With concentrated effort he briefly opened his eyes, though they fluttered shut quickly. "Everything is going to be all right. Just hang in there, honey. The ambulance is on the way."

"I wanna sit up," he mumbled and with that, his right arm flung straight up. I'd seen that kind of involuntary reaction before with people who were having seizures. My heart beat even faster. I was terrified.

I comforted my husband and told him it was crucial that he lie still. As I very carefully pulled my hand from under Tracy's head, I could see something none of us had yet noticed—blood. A pool of blood was under his head and my right hand was full of it! Within myself silent screams shattered my brain. God's grace kept me and my neighbors calm, but intense fear flowed cold through my veins at the sight of the blood.

Sirens sounded in the distance. I could barely breathe as we waited. Tracy was the love of my life, and he was suffering in front of my eyes. I was going to have to trust God completely as the pilot and believe that we were not headed for a crash landing. I didn't want to be here. I couldn't imagine such a turn in our story. I softly stroked Tracy's hair to soothe him as the ambulance pulled into the driveway.

"Dawn, are you okay?" a voice from behind me asked. My assistant, Momma Liz, had made her way from our home to my side. Her presence and comforting touch offered me strength in that moment. We watched the EMTs carefully tend to my husband and prepare him for his journey to the emergency room.

They said I could join him, so I ran toward our home with Momma Liz right behind me. I knew I had to get something, but I didn't know what. I had the sensation of spinning and being pulled by my arms, legs, and mind in a thousand different directions. The broken record in my mind shouted, "This can't be happening. This *cannot* be happening." Liz directed my steps and rounded up my purse and shoes. We quickly returned to the ambulance.

Tracy fought the restraints of the stretcher, but his movements required such precautions. I kept telling him how much the girls and I loved him and how very proud of him we were. I told him to keep thinking of our life and love for each other and our girls. Tracy was trying to communicate with me, he was trying to talk, but he could not. I could see him struggling within himself and I knew he was suffering. All I wanted to do was hold him, comfort him, release him from the bondage of excruciating pain…make everything all right. I could not. It was one of the most emotionally devastating events of my life.

My prayers to God were a combination of pleas for help and silent screams of rage. Hadn't Tracy suffered enough? Why this?

Why now? If I was a wild woman before, then this round of internal yelling and questioning surely was that of a wildly insane woman. I could not believe that after six years of perseverance and triumph Tracy was facing his death. At that moment I felt such anger at God, yet I held on to His love with every bit of myself. It doesn't seem possible to entertain such conflicting feelings in a moment. I cannot explain it, except to say that love is not logical, nor is my passionate belief in God's love.

Waiting

I waited in the hall while the emergency room doctor ran tests. "We'll be right out," he said. "It'll only take a few minutes."

I was so glad to be alone. I squatted to a fetal position, balancing myself on the balls of my feet while curling my head toward my knees. I sobbed like a baby and slowly rocked. I knew that once the girls were with me I would need to be strong. So I cried hard, purging my emotions and placing the sorrow and anger at God's feet. I could vaguely hear people walking toward me. Two nurses whispered to each other. "She is the woman whose husband is not likely to make it."

Please, dear Lord, tell me I didn't just hear what I thought I heard! Dear God! Please help me! Help us. I buried my face back into my knees as fast as I could, hoping the nurses wouldn't notice me. Not realizing I had heard them, they came to my side and offered me comfort. Did I want a chair? Did I need anything? *What could anyone possibly do for the woman whose husband is not going to make it?* I thought. I knew that for this pain in my chest, in my heart, in my soul...there was no earthly thing that could comfort me now. No soft, warm blanket. No kind words. No chicken soup. No promises spoken from human lips. Only Jesus.

Tracy's parents arrived and saw their sweet son in pain. His mother, Rose, held both hands over her mouth. Dad Hall stood with his left arm around her and his right hand on Tracy. Wayne and Rose watched their son's final hours. I watched the love of my life slip away. No words could express the sorrow of that moment. I wanted to ride off on the river of silence that flooded that stark room.

Going Home

Recently we had voted as a family to return to our old church. After devoting some time to an area church and enjoying that fellowship, we felt it was time to return to our "home." Two days later Tracy died.

I will never forget the feeling of being totally engulfed in love as I walked into that church's atrium to discuss funeral arrangements with the pastor. "Welcome home," God seemed to say to my spirit. I felt bathed in His love and attention. He had guided us back to Calvary Assembly of God in time for my husband's funeral. Even after such a twist in our story, I again felt the security of order, God's order.

More than two thousand people attended the visitation and funeral service. Complete strangers drove hours to offer their condolences and say thank you for what a wonderful inspiration my husband and I had been to them. It was quite humbling.

Tracy had made a video of himself for his funeral about a year prior to his death. He praised God for the great life he had, encouraged others to have a relationship with God, and thanked everyone for their love and friendship. It was quite beautiful. I spoke for about 15 minutes, also encouraging others to live life to its fullest, be right with God, and be ready for their own death.

When people filed by to see Tracy for the last time, they saw him dressed in his preferred uniform: his work boots, denim jeans, a John Deere cap, and a sweatshirt I had made with clouds on the front that said "God's Property."

At the graveside our friend Toni sang one of Tracy's favorite songs, "Amazing Grace." A dove was released and helium balloons floated to the heavens. The dove struggled a little before it left its cage and peacefully flew away. *How appropriate,* I thought. To me it was a beautiful symbol of Tracy's struggle before he left this world.

Malcolm Muggeridge said, "If it weren't for death, life would be unbearable." This also brings me back to some sense of order. I don't know how this life is going to turn out. I cannot protect everyone I love from illness, pain, or suffering…but I can rest in knowing that physical death is followed by eternal life. That is the order of things in God's will.

The day of the funeral and the many difficult days that followed carved out a new path. I no longer thought I could control it. I didn't even begin to presume what would come next. But each step of the way showed me God's provision. And now I find my peace and my comfort in knowing that the greeting I sensed when I entered church that day was the same greeting Tracy heard when he went to be with his Lord…welcome home…welcome home.

COMFORT FOOD FOR THOUGHT

No matter where the path leads us,
God is our home.

Lasagna Supreme

2 egg whites
1 15-ounce container fat-free
    ricotta cheese (I use Frigo)
14 ounces Healthy Choice Low-Fat
    Smoked Sausage
1 pound hamburger
8 ounces fresh mushrooms—thinly sliced
½ medium onion chopped (approximately ½ cup)
1 27.5-ounce jar spaghetti sauce (I prefer Ragu Chunky Garden Harvest)
1 16-ounce box lasagna noodles—prepared as directed on package
¾ pound fat-free mozzarella cheese (I prefer Healthy Choice)
6 tablespoons grated Parmesan cheese

Preheat oven to 350°. Spray a large saucepan and a 9 x 13-inch pan with nonfat cooking spray. Beat egg whites with ricotta cheese. Set aside. Grind up sausage in a food processor. In prepared saucepan, combine hamburger and sausage until fully cooked. Do not drain. Add mushrooms and onion. Cover and cook on low for 4 to 5 minutes. Add spaghetti sauce. Mix well. Turn off heat.

Lay 4 long lasagna noodles across the bottom of the prepared 9 x 13-inch pan. The sides of the lasagna noodles will overlap slightly. Layer the ingredients in the following order:

1½ cups meat sauce
lasagna noodles
1 cup ricotta-cheese mixture
1 cup mozzarella cheese
2 tablespoons Parmesan cheese, sprinkled
lasagna noodles
1½ cups meat sauce
lasagna noodles
1 cup ricotta-cheese mixture

1 cup mozzarella cheese

2 tablespoons Parmesan cheese, sprinkled

lasagna noodles

2 cups meat sauce

1 cup mozzarella cheese

2 tablespoons Parmesan cheese, sprinkled

Note: A little sauce will be left over.

Bake for 30 minutes. Let the dish cool a few minutes before cutting. It can be eaten immediately, refrigerated until ready to use, or frozen. (If this dish has been prepared ahead of time and frozen, bake for 45 to 55 minutes or until it is fully cooked.)

Serves: 12   Fat Grams: 4.6   Calories: 343

What's on Your Plate?

1. Have you had to find your way through grief? If you are doing so now, what brings order to your steps?

2. Are you emotionally boxing up some experiences right now? How are those boxes labeled? What are you trying to wrap up so you can move forward?

3. Are you pleased with the way you think you will be remembered? If not, what would you change?

4. Tracy was buried in a sweatshirt that said "God's Property" on the front of it. What would your sweatshirt say?

5. Do you find comfort when you think of eternal life? How does the thought of being in God's presence forever help you through your today?

God's Recipe for Purpose

Whatever you have learned or received or heard from me, or seen in me—put it into practice. And the God of peace will be with you.

PHILIPPIANS 4:9

But each man has his own gift from God; one has this gift, another has that.

1 CORINTHIANS 7:7

We were therefore buried with him through baptism into death in order that, just as Christ was raised from the dead through the glory of the Father, we too may live a new life.

ROMANS 6:4

Do not conform any longer to the pattern of this world, but be transformed by the renewing of your mind. Then you will be able to test and approve what God's will is—his good, pleasing and perfect will.

ROMANS 12:2

Honor the LORD with your wealth, with the firstfruits of all your crops; then your barns will be filled to overflowing, and your vats will brim over with new wine.

PROVERBS 3:9-10

The LORD will fulfill his purpose for me; your love, O LORD, endures forever—do not abandon the works of your hands.

PSALM 138:8

Jesus said to the woman, "Your faith has saved you; go in peace."

LUKE 7:50

Sixteen

Saying Grace
Thankful for a Future and a Hope

I thank God for second chances and new beginnings. Actually I thank Him for second chances, third chances, and fourth chances. Every time I mess up or make a mistake, He graciously forgives me, strengthens me, and provides for me. I am so grateful for such a loving God.

Can you see a second chance forming during this time? Your trial might be one that restricts your view of possible new beginnings in the future. Wherever you are in your circumstance of difficulty…that is where you can rest in God's comfort and strength. God doesn't offer such caretaking only at certain times along the way. He is there with us every step we take…whether we stumble or stand tall and walk with certainty. He is beside us.

I can look back over the years leading up to Tracy's illness and those just following his death, and I see God's hand so securely on my circumstance. God called Tracy and me to stand tall, persevere, and to rest in Him. He never said that if Tracy was not healed it would mean we were not faithful. He said He would use the pages of our story, its ups and downs, twists and turns, times of anger and times of faithfulness, to bring goodness into the world.

Personally, God was preparing me to share more about Him with people I did not know—but He did. The testimony that has come from my story, and the empathy and compassion that has grown from my sorrow, are now pieces of faith I share with others.

When I was first asked to speak at a church service I didn't feel worthy of being used by God in this manner. I quickly declined by saying, "Thank you very much, but I don't do public speaking." Within the same week another church asked me to speak. *Maybe God is trying to tell me something*, I thought, and this time I said, "I have never done public speaking, but I'll think and pray about it."

I looked at Bible scholars, teachers, and preachers I admired, such as my pastors, Chuck Swindoll, Joyce Meyer, and Billy Graham. They probably hardly ever get upset or shout at God the way I have over the past few years. I felt they were model Christians…and what they did was far out of my league. I could not measure up to such standards. Still, I kept my word and prayed about it, knowing God surely was not calling me to public speaking.

"I want to use you," I heard Him say.

Soon my prayer became a debate with God about why He couldn't or shouldn't use me. "I don't know all the books of the Bible or their order. Don't You remember me yelling at You with anger and frustration? You cannot possibly…"

"I want to use you," God interrupted.

He kept reconfirming this to me over and over again. If God wants to use you in a certain way and you want to live according to His will, arguing is pretty useless.

I now accept the opportunities God places before me. I believe my primary purpose is to inspire and encourage people, women especially. The cookbooks I've written are simply tools God is using. People will come to listen to me—Dawn Hall, the cookbook lady—whereas they might not go to listen to a pastor speak. People don't feel threatened by a cookbook lady. I can share the Word of God in a way that touches different people in different ways. It is a God thing through and through.

I chose to be obedient in the writing and the speaking, and to my surprise countless people have said that the story about my family's struggles and joys has been an inspiration to them. I believe God's hand guided me toward this calling, this purpose for my life, because He was creating an ongoing source of comfort and encouragement for me. Each time I speak to a group or share with someone one-on-one, it is affirmed that God is not only using me and my life, He is caring for me. It is beyond anything I could have imagined or planned on my own. I think of 2 Corinthians 1:3-7:

> Praise be to the God and Father of our Lord Jesus Christ, the Father of compassion and the God of all comfort, who comforts us in all our troubles, so that we can comfort those in any trouble with the comfort we ourselves have received from God. For just as the sufferings of Christ flow over into our lives, so also through Christ our comfort overflows. If we are distressed, it is for your comfort and salvation; if we are comforted, it is for your comfort, which produces in you patient endurance of the same sufferings we suffer. And our hope for you is

firm, because we know that just as you share in our
sufferings, so also you share in our comfort.

What Christ gives us, we are blessed to give to others. What
life gives us, we are privileged to share with others.

I know that right now you might be having a hard time with
life's uncertainties. I pray that you will see more and more each
day how God is using your circumstance for goodness while He
is also caring for you. Watch for His provision. When He touches
your heart, in big and little ways, rejoice and reach out to Him in
gratitude. He calls you to your purpose, and while it is unfolding,
He calls you to His side where He covers your need, your anger,
your sorrow, your questions, and your weariness with His strength
and love.

COMFORT FOOD FOR THOUGHT
*God wants to use us and
our circumstances for good.*

Melt-in-Your-Mouth Comfort, Mashed Potatoes

2 pounds baking potatoes,
    such as Idaho or Russet
3 tablespoons lite margarine
1 5-ounce can fat-free evaporated milk

    Peel and cut the potatoes into 1-inch chunks. Put the potato chunks into a large pot. Cover with salt water (use 30 percent less sodium salt). Bring potatoes and water to a full boil over high heat. Once water is at a full boil, turn heat off. Cover with lid. Let potatoes rest in the hot water for 20 minutes. (This method works every time! No need to worry about overcooking the potatoes or having them absorb too much water.)

    Drain the water.

    Microwave the milk for about 40 seconds or until warm. Add margarine to the potatoes. Mash the potatoes with a potato masher, or you can use a mixer on low speed and gradually beat in milk until smooth and creamy. Season with salt and pepper if desired.

    Serves: 8   Fat Grams: 2   Calories: 109

What's on Your Plate?

1. In what ways have you felt God calling you to serve Him?

2. Have you felt qualified to be used by God in the areas He's called you to? Do you resist God using your abilities or your inabilities? Consider one area of weakness that you can give over to God's strength to be used for His glory.

3. Meditate on 2 Corinthians 1:3-7. How has another person shared the comfort of God with you? How is God allowing you to share His comfort with others...and even with yourself?

4. In what way have you changed along this journey? Is your personal purpose clearer? Do you see God's hand on your life as you look back over the years? If this is hard for you still, spend time considering how God's hand will be on your future. Thank Him for this security and share knowledge of His love as part of your purpose.

5. Be kind to yourself. Offer yourself the nourishment of His Word. And feast on the comfort food that comes your way:

beginnings	abundance
life	giving and receiving
trust	transformation and
provision	forgiveness
wholeness	peace
community	joy
help	comfort
patience	purpose
goodness	

How to Contact the Author

Dawn Hall is the award-winning author of *Busy People's Down Home Cooking Without the Down Home Fat, Busy People's Low-Fat Cookbook,* and *Busy People's Slow Cooker Cookbook.*

She is also the host of *Cooking for Busy People,* a 30-minute television show featured on WLMB-TV. As a popular inspirational speaker, Dawn brings hope and healing to audiences across the country.

To communicate with Dawn about speaking engagements, please contact her at:

5425 Fulton Lucas Rd.
Swanton, OH 43558
Phone: (419) 826-2665
Fax: (419) 825-2700

Discover more about Dawn, her books, and her speaking ministry by visiting her website:

www.dawnhallcookbooks.com

Other Good Books
from Harvest House Publishers

Letter to a Grieving Heart
by Billy Sprague

A Simple Gift of Comfort
by Jane Kirkpatrick

Quiet Moments for Your Soul
by Steve Chapman

One-Minute Prayers for Women

A Cup of Hope
by Emilie Barnes

The Comforting Presence of God
by Nancie Carmichael

Prayers in the Storm
by Sandy Clough

HARVEST HOUSE
PUBLISHERS